Advance Praise

TURN POSSIBILITIES INTO REALITIES

In *Turn Possibilities Into Realities,* authors Lisa Marie Platske, et al, take both men and women on a profoundly moving and diverse journey of self-discovery, of what it means actually to be good to oneself, of how the ties that bind can make or break a person, and how the passionate and compassionate spark residing in our souls can spur us to action and harness our inner and outer leader. This thought provoking, poignant, frequently humorous, and inspirational book provides a closer look at the DNA of today's working woman and is a game changer; and is written for the woman who is ready to work hard and persevere, ready to swim against the tide, and already "wearing many hats" and wearing them well.

Read this creative, evocative, and collaborative effort by these dynamic and talented women, who wryly and matter of factly voice the cultural trends, dreams, fears, and pitfalls affecting the work/life balance we all strive for! It will help you reengage with an "inner voice" that may have gone quiet. It will help you redefine success and what it actually means to lead. It will help you embrace change and relinquish fear of the unknown. I wish I had this handy "travel guide" when I began my own challenging journey as an entrepreneur!

~ **Penina Rybak, Founder/CEO Socially Speaking LLC**
Author: *The NICE Reboot: A Guide to Becoming a Better Female Entrepreneur—How to Balance Your Cravings for Humanity and Technology in Today's Startup Culture*

This book is a must read. The stories of these individuals' lives are a living chronicle of our need to not stop dreaming, to authentically be present and engaged in pursuing opportunities to nurture, to perfect, and to support the dream within ourselves that will manifest in ways that positively affects the organizations and human lives we touch.

~ **Tonia Lediju**
Director of City Audits
City Services Auditor Division
Office of the Controller
City and County of San Francisco

I found Lisa Marie's book to be insightful, interesting and at the same time a very practical guide to learning to live an authentic life. It's difficult and sometimes impossible for us to see that practicality and hard work, albeit not the "burning bush" we hope for, does

TURN POSSIBILITIES INTO REALITIES

*Experts Bridge the Gap from a What If...
Into a What Is*

Created by:

Lisa Marie Platske

Featuring

Dr. Theresa Ashby

Garet Bedrosian

Patricia Bucci

Marlene Cain

Celeste Ducharme

Susan Kerby

Ann Marie Johnson

Guylaine Saint Juste

Victoria Villalba

Dedication

To all those women in the world who have taken a
leap of faith in stepping forward with a bold "yes" to
their dreams and to all those who are waiting
reluctantly that they may have the courage to step
into their calling.

TURN POSSIBILITIES INTO REALITIES

Table of Contents

Foreword

TURN POSSIBILITIES INTO REALITIES

by

Kristina Bouweiri

TURN POSSIBILITIES INTO REALITIES

*We are all faced with a series of
great opportunities disguised as impossible
situations.*

~ **Charles R. Swindoll** (1934—)
Evangelical Christian pastor, author, educator, and
radio preacher

Lisa Marie Platske's passion in life is leading others to a unique "upside" kind of thinking that helps them experience success not found in common hours. Lisa Marie's formulas and systems can guarantee success when implemented. I first met Lisa Marie at one of Oprah's weekend events, to which a mutual friend invited us to attend. Not only was it a most inspirational weekend, but I met and hit it off with a very special woman whom I've since seen in action... doing a fantastic job facilitating a major board retreat. It is said how we do one thing in life is how we do all things; Lisa Marie brings excellence to the world as she connects with others and teaches leadership skills.

Turn Possibilities into Realities is yet another bold, upside idea Lisa Marie chose to bring positive change to the world. She wisely chartered anthology contributors through myriad channels of life in an acknowledgment to those who helped turn possibilities into realities and develop their own leadership qualities. It is obvious each author was hand-picked to bring the best stories to readers. This is not another business book where you learn the theories taught in business school; it is filled with stories—each a unique journey through life's challenges, to recognize a mentor who helped make paths less burdensome and leave the reader with exclusive challenges to foster leadership skills.

You may recognize yourself in these stories, as I did, reminded of how I found my own "mentor" in Nelson Mandela. I had the great fortune of my father's career taking us to many countries, and went to school with Mandela's children—at a time when he came out to lead his country through the devastation of apartheid—a most distressing scenario for a child to experience. However, I was caught in his leadership model and learned the essence of wanting to be "part of the solution."

I was touched by the unique ways these writers revealed the leadership qualities upon which they had come to rely. There I was—in heart and mind—recalling how my own sense of adaptability was developed. My story of learning how to deal with the highs and lows of owning a business came at a young age—I had to be adaptable to changing environments every three years through my father's involvement in overseas foreign service. I experienced myriad difficult surroundings in an Amazon jungle, where your beds are built on stilts, or leaving Africa in the middle of the night, having been kicked out of the country by a new regime... surrounded by gorillas with machine guns.

I fully understood the core values each woman shared—one of them being inclusive in how I treat employees and managers, friends and associates. My own journey to leadership involved my being a minority; I learned not to see color and this value serves me well because many of my employees and customers are from other countries.

Most of this book's contributors write of life-long learning. As an "accidental entrepreneur," I was called upon to shift gears many times in my own career. As a Political Science major, I determined to follow in my dad's foreign service footsteps, but found a twist in my path and worked for a non-profit in Africa... and yet another turn being most unwillingly pushed into commission sales, and subsequently owning a limousine company. Little did I know each change required I do more than work hard to grow a company—I had to keep learning both industry and life skills. The travesty of 911 taught me to rely on seminars, book clubs, and peer groups to thrive; in the second ten years of ownership, the things I learned helped me quadruple the company.

This book is for you if you have any inclination toward leadership. Each contributor challenges you, the reader, to take action in expanding your capacity as a leader; each suggestion is as varied as the stories that precede them. You will find yourself in many of these stories, and recognize that you are more of a leader than you gave yourself credit—or find tools in these challenges to step into a larger leadership role, which you will feel more confident in claiming.

Congratulations! You are taking the first step to having the leadership skills you desire.

~ **Kristina Bouweiri**
Owner: Reston Limousine and Travel Service, Inc.
Washington DC Metropolitan Area
https://www.restonlimo.com/

Acknowledgments

I HAVE WATCHED countless women (and men) in my life take a thought—a mere, "What if... ?" and turn it into something tangible, and always wondered what happens on the journey in that person's mind to make him or her deliberately walk into uncharted territory. No map. No plotted course. Just a commitment to doing whatever it takes to make the dream a reality. My mission and purpose to create this book was to feature women who say "yes" to life and fearlessly choose to live their calling... bridging the gap from a possibility to a reality.

If you had told me when I started this project what it would take both physically and emotionally to bring this book to print, my fear may have stopped me from bringing these stories to life. I underestimated the scope and depth as well as the countless challenges that continued to surface. However, I believed in this book and its power. I trust it will change lives as the journey has changed mine.

I would like to acknowledge the following people for their support through the process.

Lorraine Bosse-Smith, managing project editor, for her dedication to the completion of the project and her attention to details;

Jo Della Penna, for listening to every challenge during the journey and encouraging me to stay the course;

Sheri Granneman, for being the glue that kept all of the pieces and parts of the project moving forward;

Pamela Herman, for believing in me and wanting more for me;

Cathy Jennings, for serving as my Upside Impact Partner (UIP); being both cheerleader and confidante;

Adrienne Moch, for friendship and last minute edits;

Tyler Tichelaar, for your flexibility and eagle-eye proofreading;

Anna Weber, founder of Voices In Print, for her loving support and personal desire to help me create (and deliver) the best product possible for the writers—and readers;

Becky Whatley, for being a champion for my business and every project I've ever engaged in;

Viki Winterton, for your dedication to authors in getting their message out into the world; and

All of the women who chose lovingly and openly to share their stories.

Know that my heart dances with gratitude for my loving and supportive husband, Jim Platske. He makes me want to show up as the best version of myself as he believes in my ability to turn possibilities into realities. I am proud to be called his wife. This book would not have been completed without his steady stream of encouragement and love.

Finally, I would like to acknowledge YOU—the reader. This book was written with your journey in mind.

Introduction

TURN POSSIBILITIES INTO REALITIES

by

Lisa Marie Platske

Turn Possibilities into Realities

*If you'll not settle for anything less
than your best, you will be amazed at what you
can accomplish in your lives.*

~ **Vince Lombardi** (1913—1970)
American Hall of Fame football coach

Leadership is ultimately about influence—those who have it and those who don't. Our culture, education, family life, siblings, friends, peers, and external environment shape and mold us into the human beings we are today. I've discovered through my own journey of ups and downs that although all of us possess some inherent leadership qualities, "born leaders" are people who have evolved through diligent and consistent effort.

Every opportunity gives us a lesson we can use in the future, and if used properly, these lessons serve as the stepping stones to pave our way to a bright new possibility. Know that not everyone reaps the great rewards from the opportunities that have been presented to them. Whether or not you believe you are born with leadership prowess, influence is something that can be easily lost, requiring us to develop further or face becoming irrelevant. In my observation, you can wait to be developed or take an active role in the change process by seeking out people and places to learn from: mentors, boards, peers, or mastermind groups.

The Leadership Journey

YES, LEADERS ARE life-long learners. They seek opportunities to grow and expand, and it reflects through the choices they've made their entire life. Since pre-school, they've sought to achieve, master, and glean new aptitudes, skills, and knowledge to move them to the next goal—the next big thing.

Since we all get the ability to develop the leader within us, where we are on our journey doesn't matter, nor does how old we are or what our title or background is. What does matter is whether we're focused on intentionally growing the unique set of gifts, talents, and abilities that are ours and ours alone. Do you find yourself courageously taking control in the driver's seat or sitting in the back going along for the ride?

My career in federal law enforcement began over twenty years ago and allowed me to take a journey like no other. With winding roads and incredible peaks to climb, it was one heck of a ride. I vividly recall experiences like sitting on the tarmac as the Concorde took off, rumbling engines shaking my unmarked vehicle, and a presidential detail with the New York Police Department over the 4th of July. I remember digging through cargo in containers from across the world, giving me the unique opportunity to witness some of the most jaw-dropping and sometimes awe-inspiring things on this planet. These experiences have also enabled me to get up-close and personal with leaders who have impacted public policy, social justice, and scores of world issues. Being in their presence has brought out the best in me and allowed me to find the best in who I am.

As for the future, your task is not to foresee it, but to enable it.

~ **Antoine de Saint-Exupery** (1900—1944)
French aviator and writer

Whether you're looking at micro-businesses, small to medium size enterprises, world giants, government, education, or non-profits, each organization relies on exceptional leadership to move the mission forward and impact and re-design the destiny of those who enter its sphere of influence. It's the long-term impact, not the short-term wins, that changes the landscape of the world, one opportunity at a time. And, if the organization values people and relationships and weaves them into the purpose and vision of the institution, its capacity for greatness—and producing great leaders—increases.

Great leaders lead with the soul of the organization at the forefront, which enables others to grow. As you look closer at what leaders do, say, and how they behave, they know no one wakes up and says, "Today is the day I'm going to fail." Everyone wants to succeed at all times and in big ways. Most people wonder how they can bring positive change into their lives and turn a possibility into a reality. Yet, if you get caught up in the challenges of leadership, you'll fail to recognize the incredible celebrations that occur each day.

All people have the ability within them to become great leaders if they take their own gifts, talents, skills, and abilities and apply them to the ideas being shared inside these pages.

One of the most exciting pieces of this project is that these women aren't just doers and achievers; they're heart-felt leaders who have made a significant impact on the world with their ideas and presence. Their decisions have changed lives, and yet they're each incredibly humble and reserved about the impact they've created.

It is in your hands to create a better world for all who live in it.

~ **Nelson Mandela** (1918—2013)
South African statesman

The women in this book have all made a significant contribution to the world as a result of their leadership. Our backgrounds are varied, and our stories are the stories of the world. We represent women of different races, backgrounds, upbringings, and experiences. Some of us have come from places of comfort and wealth, while others have experienced great hardship and managed to rise to the top. Their individual contributions to this book will allow you, the reader, a snapshot of their journeys, and we are entrusting you with these stories as an opportunity for growth and transformation.

If you are like me, you will likely want to skim through the book before settling down to read it in its entirety. However, I lovingly suggest you read the book one chapter at a time, processing the message and focusing on the *Leadership Challenge* offered by each writer at the end of her chapter, knowing every word was chosen with you and your journey in mind.

> *It's not enough what I did in the past — there is also the future.*

> ~ **Rita Levi-Montalcini** (1909—2012)
> Italian scientist, senator, Nobel Prize winner

When I began this project, the intention of *Turn Possibilities into Realities* had a straight-forward objective: encourage others deliberately to shape their own futures by reflecting on the stories of others who have gone before them and taken the road less traveled. I believe the threads of life, this moment in time, bring us into contact with others' experiences and can help us weave a more brilliant tapestry of our own life story.

Getting to this place, where you actually have a

book in your hands, has been no ordinary feat. Much like the title of this book, I began with a "What if . . . ?" What if I gathered a group of women who understood the power of choice, direction, commitment and consistent action, and asked them to share what happens when you move from having a great idea to turning it into something tangible—and that sweet taste of victory?

What if readers were challenged with a series of action items on how to move from their own "what if" or possibility into taking consistent action? Hmm . . . what if?!?

One benefit of risking failure. . .
the risk of success.

~ **Sam Parker** (1965—)
American businessperson and writer

I get what it's like when you feel paralyzed with wanting to do "something more" but not ever moving past the idea and discovering what it is and how it would happen. And, I want you to put this book down knowing you can have anything you want and anything is possible once you make a choice, move in the direction you want, step into commitment, and take consistent action.

Now, let's get started. First, I encourage you to sit back and get comfortable. Ah, yes. that's it. Be present to what's about to unfold within the pages of this book. One of the pillars of leadership that you'll hear me share is to *Start with the End in Mind*. So, I challenge you to begin with why you are reading this book. You will get what you believe you will find. Clarify your intentions about what you want to get out of the investment of time that you are putting into this. Remember, consistency is priceless. If you will sit for just ten minutes every day, focusing on your intention with the leadership challenge, your intuition will guide you to your own reality and provide you with endless opportunities to influence your own world.

Great love is here for you! As always, we remain authentically connected.

Chapter 1

LEADERSHIP FROM THE INSIDE OUT

by

Garet Bedrosian

Leadership from the Inside Out

Whatever affects one directly,
affects all indirectly.
I can never be what I ought to be
until you are what you ought to be.
This is the interrelated
structure of reality.

~ Martin Luther King (1929—1968)
Humanitarian

I live an inspired life, and sometimes I have to pinch myself to make sure it's real. I am writing this chapter from my home in beautiful San Diego, which I was able to purchase through my entrepreneurial endeavors.

Twenty-eight years ago, I became a licensed psychotherapist and am passionate about somatic and energetic healing, relationships, and sexuality. I have had the honor of helping literally thousands of individuals and couples through the years by sharing the work that I love.

I am a leader in my profession and am privileged to teach locally, nationally, and internationally. I am the executive director of the Southern California Institute of Bioenergetic Analysis and a member of the International Bioenergetic Faculty. I am a keynote speaker and author, and I lead relationship workshops based on Imago Relationship Theory and sexual healing. In 2014, I was awarded San Diego Clinical Social Worker of the year.

Personally, I have a loving and connected relationship, an eclectic group of friends from all around the world, and a supportive family. I am healthy, active, and belong to a worldwide dance community. I travel to interesting and intriguing places and connect with others who love to dance as much as I do; Argentine Tango is my latest obsession.

I could not have imagined any of this when I was younger. Learning how to express myself in a fuller, more authentic way has been my bane and my blessing.

Dancing to a different drummer, while fun, is also a challenge. I grew up in a family where, from an early age, I felt as if I didn't fit in. I was out of step with the people around me. I wasn't brave enough to stand out, and I wasn't confident enough to fit in.

Now I realize that although my parents loved me, I lacked attuned support, the kind of attention that children need to feel they are seen, accepted, and belong in the world. Because my family was not able to give me that type of support, I suppressed the most vibrant and expressive parts of myself. I was an alive and adventurous child, often found climbing trees, exploring the woods behind my house, or riding my bike beyond my parents' boundaries—repeatedly hearing, "Be quiet, be still, behave," or "There you go with those crocodile tears," which shut down my emotions and my expressiveness.

My paternal grandmother, Anna Bozigian, was my saving grace and influenced my life in profound ways. She died when I was six years old, but her legacy is woven into the fabric of my being.

Her life had been defiled in the 1915 Armenian genocide. The Ottoman Empire massacred one and a half million Armenians; her husband and children were among those killed. Alone, Anna was able to escape to the mountains of France. Eventually, she met and married Aristokes Bedrosian. He came from a neighboring village where he had narrowly escaped after witnessing the murders of his wife and children. Anna inspired him. She was strong—a survivor—and she pushed him to take a leap of faith. Together, they gathered what little they had and made their way across the world to North America.

In the U.S., my grandmother was highly regarded in her new community. As a healer and a brilliant entrepreneur, she created opportunities for her three sons. Her green thumb was legendary, as were her other talents. My grandmother was a midwife, cared for the sick, amassed real estate, opened a small grocery store, and helped others achieve their dreams through financial loans.

When I was six, she was my heroine. Back then, I didn't know about my grandmother's perils or her many accomplishments. All I knew was that she adored me, comforted me, encouraged me, and let me know I was special.

For many years after her death, I felt lost. Because I was their first born and female child, my parents frequently discouraged and restricted my venturesome spirit, thinking that was the best approach. To keep me safe from a dangerous world, they attempted to impart conventional beliefs and wisdoms, which were not generally in line with my nature. My soul expressions and deep longings found refuge deep inside. As a result, I appeared timid and afraid to the world. A saving grace was my connection with my siblings, and through our very active fantasy life, I was able to keep the excitement of future possibilities alive. Together we imagined and enacted adventures we would have once we grew up, and we longed for a time when we could make our own choices. As youngsters, we would imagine ourselves skydiving, scuba diving, and horseback riding.

I am thrilled to tell you that I manifested each of those adventures and am immensely grateful for those early imaginings. They helped preserve the most precious parts of me.

Educationists should build the capacities of the spirit of inquiry, creativity, entrepreneurial and moral leadership among students and become their role model.

~ **A.P.J. Abdul Kalam** (1931—)
Eleventh President of India

Learning Beyond the Classroom

MANY PEOPLE BLOSSOM in school, but that was not my experience. My educational experiences were stifling. I know now I am a kinesthetic learner with a wandering mind who needs an active, experiential learning environment. Instead, because I couldn't follow the didactic lectures and

7

classroom reading, I was shamed, shut down, and told I wasn't smart enough to go to college. I was made to take business-oriented classes, which bored me and further discouraged my creativity. This experience solidified my belief that I must be stupid; it was my only explanation for failure, so I stopped trying.

Once I was away from that disparaging academic setting, I pursued other interests more suited to my nature. I had always been fascinated by people, places, and things, longing for adventure. I had inherited my grandmother's green thumb and studied horticulture, filling my home with hundreds of plants. I studied classical guitar, photography, and yoga. I danced, traveled, hiked, biked, camped, and rode horses. Being active and in nature fed my soul but accentuated the split between my internal self and outside persona. My life looked great on the outside, but internally, I remained in anguish. I was not living my life purpose and had no idea how to heal that crevasse.

In retrospect, I believe my grandmother's courageous spirit was an unconscious force in my life, but it took some maturity and life lessons for me to embrace it. My life experiences taught me that when we are physically, emotionally, mentally, and spiritually aligned with our life purpose and desires, opportunities for manifestation become available.

When the pupil is ready, the master arrives.

~ Zen Proverb

I TRULY BELIEVE when you are ready for change, the universe responds. I began to meet people who encouraged me to pursue a different life. Despite my terror about not being smart enough to succeed, I returned to school. My painful discontent became my gift and brought me to the study of psychology and sociology. I finally began to understand my angst, and from that point, I couldn't get enough of learning. My mind absorbed my interests in a new way.

I came to understand and appreciate my empathic nature, which awakened a desire to help others bridge that disconcerting gap between their authentic expression and the imposed persona they were living. I didn't want anyone else to feel so alone and suffer with this core pain.

Your task is not to seek for love,
but merely to seek and find all the barriers
within yourself that you
have built against it.

~ **Rumi** (1207—1273)
Sufi Poet

Honoring my free spirit, internal wisdom, intuition, and curiosities has taken a lifetime—each experience chipping away the rough edges of my protective armor as I have been on a quest for wholeness, peace, joy, passion, and self-love.

The Healing Process

BECOMING CONSCIOUS OF who we are today as adults and what we need requires intention. We can easily distract ourselves and even avoid uncomfortable or painful feelings. We'll encounter a million ways to do that. Many of those distractions are even encouraged in our society. This is significant because being vulnerable and mindful goes against the mainstream and definitely against the traditional teachings on leadership. We are involved in a paradigm shift about leading, relationships, and living our soul's purpose.

10

Making a lot of money isn't enough, neither is dictating from the top down about the way things should be. Settling for a life partner who looks good on paper or is better than being alone doesn't cut it. Working in a job that doesn't satisfy a deep yearning for creative expression will never fill the void.

Becoming inspired and inspirational requires working from the inside out. First we need to be attuned to our own needs, desires, and challenges to know how best to achieve our life purpose. Once we become aligned with our authentic nature, we can create a congruent vision. From that perspective, we can inspire others to become whom they are meant to be.

As a somatic, energetic, and relational therapist, I emphasize the benefits of embodiment and connection. When we experience emotional wounding or trauma as children, we can numb ourselves to deny painful feelings. This type of defense causes severe chronic muscular tension. Sometimes as adults, we reinforce that defense when we are working or living in ways that are out of alignment with our nature. Mainstream society values production over following our bliss, so this defense gets reinforced.

11

You only have to let the soft animal of your
body love what it loves.

~ **Mary Oliver** (1935—)
American Poet

Equine Radar

WE CAN LEARN so much about the topic of embodiment by being with horses. Horses are prey animals, and their survival from carnivorous predators depends on their instincts. They usually belong to herds, whether that is two or twenty, and each herd has a leader. The leader is the one most embodied and attuned to himself, the herd, the environment, and signs of endangerment.

When humans interact with them, horses tune in and assess the degree of danger. They gauge safety through a sense of emotional, physical, and mental congruence. For instance, if the human is nervous or afraid but denying it, the horse will not feel safe and will try to get away. Horses have no judgments, so their feedback is purely about safety, not about worth or lovability. Using feedback from horses can offer valuable insight and enlightenment that can then be transferred to other areas of your life.

12

In a recent Equus session, a woman (whom I shall name, Elizabeth) was challenged with feelings of not being heard or respected. She felt no one in her life took her needs or requests seriously, and believed she had to do everything herself. In the round pen with a horse, the part Elizabeth played in this ongoing struggle became clear. The instructions I gave were to get the horse to change gaits as it moved around the round pen.

Although this was Elizabeth's intention, the horse was not complying and it triggered myriad similar feelings of powerlessness she had described in her life outside the round pen. The exercise helped Elizabeth discover was giving mixed messages.

Feelings of dejection had their origins in Elizabeth's childhood; she had been energetically and unconsciously protecting herself from feeling hurt and sorrow. The early childhood experiences left her feeling neglected and unimportant. Even though Elizabeth's adult mind was open to changing this belief, her unconscious mind was holding on for dear life. This holding and suppression was chronic and unconscious.

As we explored this early wounding, Elizabeth was able verbally and physically to express her feelings and release some of the physical restrictions. The energetic work helped a courageous woman reclaim her own value in a more full bodied way and become more congruently aligned with her desires. She began the exercise again with a newfound commitment.

Elizabeth stood in the center of the round pen and was able consciously to raise and lower her energy to communicate what she wanted. The horse followed her lead, and at the conclusion of the session, showed its trust by following her around the pen without a lead line, similar to a dog following its owner without a leash. She was exhilarated. Elizabeth experienced a sense of herself as a powerful leader.

Living the Possibilities

WHAT DOES BEING an inspiring leader really mean? It means being so in tune with yourself that no emotional static gets in the way of connecting with another. It means being fully present in the relationship. It means holding the person's highest self and potential in mind at all times. It means listening to what someone is saying, hearing a person's desires and the challenges, and then reflecting what you hear. In essence, it is using your nonjudgmental, equine radar. Achieving this outcome is more challenging if you are not clear and congruent within yourself.

14

*Life's challenges are not supposed to
paralyze you; they're supposed to help you
discover who you are.*

~ Bernice Johnson Reagon (1942—)
Songtalker, singer, composer, scholar,
and social activist

Although leadership often means offering
support, inspiration sometimes requires you to
challenge the other. For some of us, change can be
scary whether we desire it or not, and resistance
can be a means of protection. We might not expect
or know how to accept support, guidance,
patience, or compassion. In that case, we may have
an unconscious self-sabotaging belief and behavior
at play. We may stay stuck or unhappy because it
is familiar, instead of feeling that we will be all
right whether things work out or not.

The unknown can create fear and anxiety. If we
don't feel connected with ourselves and are not
rooted in a confidence about our worth, we can
confuse or distract ourselves and believe the
obstacles are legitimate.

In essence, walking through our own fears
provides us with the confidence that we can
support others as they face their fears. Being an

15

example of living the possibility, despite the barriers, is inspiring. Asking for and allowing others to support you on your journey is crucial; otherwise, you will not truly understand the value of that guidance and then not value what you have to offer. Creating that space for another, and gently but firmly helping to tolerate feelings that are inevitable when pushing against a growth edge, is loving compassion. Empathize with the pain of the struggle, but believe in the person's highest self. If you can hold that delicate balance, then you will be an inspirational leader worth following.

Leadership Challenge

I invite you to answer a few questions and then assess the type of action that would most support your growth as an Inside-Out Leader:

Who were the most inspiring people in your life beginning in childhood?

What about them inspired you? Why? How?

What have been your biggest challenges— beginning in childhood—to becoming your most authentic self?

What have been your most celebrated experiences?

What scares you and keeps you from achieving your truest desires? Don't just settle for the first answer... the fear of failure, fear of success, fear of speaking in public, fear of rejection, or judgment, etc. Imagine those are the portals into a deeper knowing about your core self.

What do you imagine would help you overcome those fears?

If you imagined being free from those restrictions, what would your life look like? Who would you be? What would you be doing? Who would be in your closest circles? How would you be spending your time?

What type of coach or mentor would bring you the most compatible, comprehensive and growth-producing outcome?

Congratulations! You are on your way to understanding Inside-Out Leadership. Now share your insights with someone.

NOTES:

Chapter 2

LIVE THE LIFE OF YOUR DREAMS

by

Patricia Bucci

Live the Life of Your Dreams

The biggest adventure you can take is to live the life of your dreams.

~ **Oprah Winfrey** (1954 -   )
Influential African American talk show host,
producer, actress, and philanthropist

I learned from an early age our attitudes and beliefs shape our destinies. Like many people, I grew up in a dysfunctional family. My father left when I was eight years old, and my mother was a manic depressive, who suffered from paranoid delusions. I was the eldest of four girls, all born within four years. We had very little money as my mother struggled to support the four of us, with minuscule support from my father. Our home was chaotic. However, during my mother's manic phases, our family was called upon to share some amazing experiences from which I learned many great lessons, most importantly: we are not victims of circumstances, and we ultimately have control and responsibility for our own destiny.

As I grew up, I spent significant time with my maternal grandmother. She and I were close, and she was one of my greatest supporters, mentors, and friends. She believed in me, and from her I developed a strong faith in God, a determination to succeed, and a conviction that anything was possible.

From the first grade, I knew I was going to be a teacher. I pursued, and later lived, that dream every day of my life. I have always had a passion for helping others succeed, and I instinctively knew at a young age teachers have a tremendous opportunity to impact children profoundly. Having a challenging life growing up, I truly appreciated the teachers in my life who made a difference because they cared, believed in me, and pushed me to succeed. Their gifts were priceless.

I recently retired after a successful thirty-two-year career in public education. During my career, I had the joy of teaching fourth, seventh, and eighth grades, as well as high school. I was a supervisor, assistant principal, and finished my career as a high school principal. You could say my life was somewhat serendipitous. Very little of my life was intentionally planned, yet good things happened to me because of my excellent work

22

ethic, natural ability to connect, and the support of loving people. I was an optimist and a leader—and still am to this day!

Along the road, I learned many lessons through my experiences and the many people who have touched my life. Consequently, I determined six C's essential for success and turning *any* possibility into reality.

Clarity

*Formulate and stamp indelibly on
your mind a mental picture of yourself
succeeding. Hold this picture tenaciously.
Never permit it to fade.
Your mind will seek to develop the picture...
Do not build obstacles
in your imagination.*

~ **Norman Vincent Peale** (1898—1993)
Minister and author of
The Power of Positive Thinking

We cannot make any possibility a reality if we have not defined the reality we seek to achieve. All of us need a sense of purpose. We will not have clarity around our sense of purpose until we clearly define what it is we want. What is *your* purpose? How can *you* make a difference? Your

23

dream is fueled by your passion for pursuing what you really want and what gives purpose and meaning to your life. Be clear and set a mental picture of success and do not let self-doubt hinder your progress along the way.

Confidence

Everything that happens to you is a reflection of what you believe about yourself.
We cannot outperform our level of self-esteem.
We cannot draw to ourselves more than we think we are worth.

~ **Rev. Lyanla Vanzant** (1953—)
New York Times best-selling author; from her book
Peace from Broken Pieces

Confidence in one's abilities, talents, and skills leads to the development of a healthy self-esteem. We can achieve little in life if we do not believe in ourselves and our capacity for success. My educational background as an undergraduate was in early childhood education. Learning about the stages of child development and the essential needs of all human beings helped me to examine my own life and to identify the missing pieces. I knew I needed to be whole if I was going to help others succeed. My passion was to help every child

24

I taught to realize their own potential and unique gifts. Before I could do that for others, I had to do it for myself.

To be confident, we need to develop clarity about who we are. Identifying our strengths, abilities, and the talents that make us unique is essential to our success. We need to know who we are and what we have to offer this world. We cannot be held back by our challenges. We cannot let fear paralyze us in pursuit of our dream. Taking risks is essential, and we must willingly learn from our mistakes and failures.

I believe confidence is especially important for women, as we spend so much of our lives in service to others. Many women who lack a strong sense of who they are become people pleasers in order to obtain the acceptance and approval they are not able to give themselves. When we have not learned to say no to those things that do not align with our goals, plans, and priorities—afraid of disappointing others—we negatively impact our relationships as we become overwhelmed and resentful. We all have a limit to how much of ourselves we can give away.

Develop a strong sense of confidence in your skills, talents, and abilities. This will lead to the development of a healthy self-esteem, which is essential to overall success in life—the ability to take that possibility, or dream, and make it your reality.

Commitment

All successful people, men and
women, are big dreamers.
They imagine what their futures could be, ideal
in every respect,
and then they work every day toward their
distant vision, that goal or purpose.

~ **Brian Tracy** (1944—)
Leadership training and development coach

Without commitment, a dream remains just that... a dream. To bring our dreams to fruition, we need to set goals, create plans, and then take the necessary actions to make them a reality. Once we do this, we can set our priorities and commit to using our time toward achieving our dreams.

I have always taken every commitment I assumed and given 100 percent. On the surface, this may appear admirable, yet if we say yes to too many things, we can quickly and easily become overwhelmed, stressed, and frustrated. Caring for a husband and two children, overseeing the running of our household, driving carpools, assisting my husband with his business, working a full-time job while engaging in professional development, serving my church and community and teaching religious education, serving on the pastoral counsel, as well as a variety of outreach efforts, and visiting and caring for extended families and friends—I often ran myself ragged and then wondered why I couldn't do all of those jobs to my satisfaction. I was last on my list and had no time or energy for myself. This is a dangerous place to be. I eventually had to learn to say "no."

As women, many of us find ourselves in this place. We drift through our lives and lose sight of our dreams, often living out the dreams of others. We become disconnected from ourselves and can't help but feel as though something is missing. We lose the passion that ignited our drive. In fact, we are no longer in the driver's seat, but rather in a boat that's lost its engine, adrift among the waves. We ride the waves and hope for the best. And like me, if you are hardworking, optimistic, and grateful, you may be OK. But, is OK enough for any of us? Don't we deserve a lot more?

You must not lose sight of who you are. To live a full and complete life, having a dream, creating a plan, taking action, and continuing to grow is paramount. You must create that space for yourself. You must commit to yourself by remaining clear in what you want and where you are going. If you have lost your passion and the dream has become an illusion, you need to re-ignite the passion that fuels your dreams and motivates your action toward fulfilling those dreams. Unless you commit to caring for yourself, you will have little left to give to others.

*We cannot seek achievement for ourselves
and forget about progress and prosperity for
our community.
Our ambitions must be broad
enough to include the aspirations
and needs of others,
for their sakes and for our own.*

~ **Cesar Chavez** (1927—1993)
Union leader and labor organizer

For many of us, our dreams are built around service to others. During my career, my service was to children, parents, and colleagues. I enjoyed almost every aspect of educational service, and I believe we are all responsible for serving others. We cannot effectively serve unless we know what another needs, and this requires us to open our eyes to the world around us and form authentic connections with others.

From my mother, I learned the importance of community service and fighting for the rights of others. I had some amazing experiences that taught me the impact our lives have on our world. My mother was a strong political activist, heavily involved in the Civil Rights Movement of the 1960s, and actively involved in the fair housing movement. Despite the many protests of my grandmother, my mother loaded my sisters and me into the car and drove us to Washington, DC. I remember standing among the cheering crowd in fear and awe as Martin Luther King, Jr. delivered his "I Have a Dream" speech on the steps of the Lincoln Memorial. As an eight-year old I remember looking at the crowd around me—for the first time in my life I had some understanding of what being a minority felt like; the crowd was mostly black.

Shortly after this historic day, my mother signed a fair-housing pledge. Our small blue collar community was outraged by my mother's actions. We awoke one morning to find the words "nigger lover" sprawled in black spray paint on the side of our home, in clear sight of all who drove by. We were terrified and shortly after moved, as life in our neighborhood became unbearable. A few years later, the Civil Rights Act was passed, schools were integrated, and slowly blacks were able to buy homes in neighborhoods once inhabited solely by whites. While the hatred experienced was personally horrifying, it was gratifying to know our actions contributed to making a difference in the lives of so many.

Our experiences shape who we become. I was privileged to be a part of events that eventually changed the lives of many. Through them, I learned the importance of fighting for those with no voice, and how sometimes standing up for what you believe involves courage and has consequences you must be willing to assume.

Helping another is the quickest way to make yourself feel better. When you give, you receive the greatest gifts in your life, most especially the authentic connections you make in the process. So many people feel hopeless and stuck, but through your connection with them, you can be the one person who ignites the fire of possibility and provides the support along the path to a new reality.

Communication

*So when you are listening to
somebody, completely, attentively, then you are
listening not only to the words, but also to the
feeling of what is being conveyed, to the whole
of it, not part of it.*

~ **Jiddu Krishnamurti** (1895—1986)
Indian-born speaker and writer

Community and communication share the same root, *communis*, which means something in common. We cannot build community without effective communication. Effective communication focuses on what we have in common, not what separates us. We separate ourselves from others when we make judgments or assumptions about who they are or what they do.

I could not even begin to count all of the communications I have observed or been engaged in that ultimately led to misunderstandings. While communication encompasses a variety of discreet skills, the most common misunderstandings I have seen resulted from a lack of committed listening. Instead of listening in the present, we tend to allow our judgments, assumptions, biases, perceptions, or past experiences to cast a shadow over the communication, thus blocking our ability to really hear the message. We may attach meaning to something said or done, which in no way reflects the intended message. At other times, we may make assumptions about the motives of others based on prior experiences that have nothing to do with the present reality.

So much of our success and relationships with others is dependent upon our ability to be fully present in conversations, really listening and asking questions for clarifications, and resisting the temptation to make assumptions or judgments about others' motives. For many of us, listening

31

more and speaking less is challenging and a skill that requires consistent attention and practice to achieve.

I learned this lesson the hard way. As a teacher, and later as an administrator, I was so passionate about the success of all of my students. I was committed to making the foundational changes our school needed to prepare our students for the rapidly changing world of the 21st century. My passion and desire to forge ahead as a teacher and administrator often interfered with my ability really to listen to those affected by the changes I was seeking to make. I assumed they were unwilling to change when, in reality, they feared their own ability to succeed in a new paradigm. They did not feel heard, and interpreted my response as a lack of caring. I finally understood John C. Maxwell's adage, "People do not care how much you know, until they know how much you care."

The best way to demonstrate you care is truly to listen. You must suspend your own judgments and assumptions, and willingly acknowledge your own experiences and biases as they relate to the present. When you are successful in doing this, you have truly communicated your care and concern. Clear communication builds community.

Compassion

*Love and compassion are
necessities, not luxuries. Without them,
humanity cannot survive.*

~ **Dalai Lama** (1935-)
Tibetan Buddhist monk

We do not really love, care, or connect with any other person at a deep level without compassion. Compassion is one's ability to understand or empathize with another's suffering. When we feel compassion for others, we seek to understand and alleviate their pain. Though our lives are wonderful gifts, they are not without suffering and pain. Our ability to feel compassion demonstrates our love and genuine concern for others. Compassion is one of the greatest connectors.

Compassion must weave its way through all aspects of your life. Not only must you have compassion for others in order to be successful, but you must have compassion for yourself. You are going to make mistakes, and at times, feel shame for things you have done, or failed to do. If you cannot feel compassion for your failings, you will not receive the gift of learning from your mistakes. Instead, you will become so focused on self-flagellation and negative self-talk that you will miss the opportunity to glean new insights for

33

your future actions, becoming stuck and doomed to repeat your mistakes. Don't set yourself up for future failure because it affects your passion and motivation to pursue your purpose and live your dream. Allow compassion to permeate all areas of your life.

Practice an Attitude of Gratitude

Happiness cannot be traveled to, owned,
earned, worn, or consumed.
Happiness is the spiritual experience of living
every minute with love, grace, and gratitude.

~ **Denis Waitley** (1933—)
American motivational speaker and writer

ALTHOUGH NOT ONE of the six C's, I believe the practice of gratitude is the greatest gift we can give to ourselves and our world. When we are grateful for all of the people, events, and circumstances in our lives, we send out positive energy to our universe and attract positive energy back to ourselves. The practice of gratitude sets us up for success in all areas of our life. Practicing the six C's then becomes automatic.

Think of all the things for which you are grateful. When you come from a place of gratitude, you come from a place of abundance. When you feel abundant, you have no limit to what you can give back to the universe. Limitless possibilities become realities in your life. May all your dreams come true!

Leadership Challenge

1) Start each day by creating a gratitude list. Take just five minutes to create your initial list. Then, each day review your list and add at least five more people, possibilities, circumstances, events, or experiences for which you are grateful. You will be amazed at the change this will make in your life!

2) Review each of the six C's for success. Which area needs more attention? Be sure you are clear on what you want in *your* life. Define *your* purpose. Visualize *your* dream and commit to making it a reality by setting *your* daily, weekly, monthly, and annual goals, followed by the plans and actions you will take.

NOTES:

Chapter 3

JUST BE YOU!

by

Theresa M. Ashby, Ph.D.

Just Be You!

An eagle is still an eagle,
even if it finds itself in a cage.

~ **C. Kang** (1969—)
Physician

Few things are more unsettling than believing you are a failure, thinking your life is going the wrong way, and feeling like an outsider. That was me! As early as grade school, I recognized something was different about me. At the time, I was not able to see this in a favorable light. Consequently, I grew up learning to feel like a disappointment, unable to meet the expectations of the world at large. The passage of time did little to disabuse me of the notion I was simply "less than." In fact, things turned from bad to worse. I felt angry because others around me didn't seem to experience the ugliness of life. Yet somehow, I embraced my optimism. I found the courage and perseverance to rise above the challenges I faced. I was a resilient child. As a result, I believe adversity ultimately propels us forward, and we find the peaks of our successes are commensurate with the depths of our struggles.

At some point, I recognized I alone was responsible for creating my own path. Perhaps the critical moment was when I accepted that my own worth and intelligence, by definition, must come from within, and my greatest barriers came from being unable to accept the disparity between what the world *told* me I was, and what I *knew* I was. But first, let me share some of my journey with you.

Hard Knocks of School

ELEMENTARY SCHOOL CERTAINLY did not leave me with fond memories. Fifth grade was especially difficult when it came to math and reading. I was plagued with the reputation of having lower than average intelligence... all based upon standardized tests. Having been sentenced to the Blue Jay reading group for slow readers, I sought some reassurance from one of our loving church members about what all of this meant for me and my future. She patted me on my knee and gently broke the news, "Honey, if you are in the Blue Jay group, you are not smart enough to make it, and you will never amount to anything in this world. Just hope you find yourself a good husband." Ouch! I was only ten-years old at the time and decided school was not for me.

40

*I know nothing in the world that has
as much power as a word.
Sometimes I write one, and I look at it,
until it begins to shine.*

~ **Emily Dickinson** (1830—1886)
American poet

But the show must go on! I was off to the academy for grades eight through twelve. As though determined to prove a church member right, I continued to underperform academically and was presumably looking for a husband. Yet, neither one of those concepts really fit me well. I struggled with an identity crisis, which I eventually resolved, but those words have stayed with me forever.

Misfit in Life

IMAGINE IF YOU can... my counting down the days until I could graduate from the academy, with no plans for further education. In spite of everything I had already endured, I would need to suffer one final and horrid injustice prior to moving to the next phase of my life: six months before graduation, my older brother, Richard, was killed in a car accident. Understandably, this

41

tragedy put me into a tailspin of pain and negativity that left me even further outside of the bounds of normal than I was already feeling. Whereas before I had felt only peripherally estranged from polite academy life, I now felt as though no one would ever understand me, and this separation deepened my long-standing sense of being different. Did I fail to mention I was one of very few kids at the academy who had to work for my tuition? Being a student who worked at the Harris Pines Mill hauling lumber set me even further apart from the better-off kids; likewise, a young girl doing the type of physical labor the mill required was also viewed with suspicion by the mill workers. At the end of the day, no place felt like home, including inside my own skin.

After graduation, still wracked with the grief of my brother's death, I drifted like a lost soul at sea, finding refuge in unfulfilling relationships and jobs for which I had limited passion. In spite of everything, I was successful in professional pursuits. In fact, I became one of the youngest call center managers at the bank within only two years of starting the job... leaving me with a modicum of hope that perhaps things were looking up professionally.

My personal life was another matter entirely, however. Because I felt like an outsider for so long,

I was susceptible to the charms of anyone who would have me. A short string of unmemorable relationships ensued. In hindsight, I recognize the lion's share of responsibility for those inter-personal mishaps lay with me. How can one reasonably expect to love and be loved fully when one's self-knowledge is so limited? I had yet to uncover that the state of being a misfit could be turned to my advantage. One more pivotal life event was required to open my eyes to my own potential.

Life Lessons

UNFORTUNATELY, THE BANK where I was a manager merged with another bank; my position was eliminated. I was between lackluster relationships, and I had no plan. That's right—no plan, no money, and no home. I ended up car camping, which sounds better than the truth... I was homeless. I was able to work odd jobs cleaning homes, painting house interiors, and doing yard work so I could make my car, cell phone, and mailbox payments. My next move may astonish you: I decided to sign up at the local junior college.

Why the renewed interest in school? Don't worry, I had none! Instead, I had a clever survival plan whereby I could use the gym showers for only

$5.00 a semester. I also found the college parking lot was a great place to park my car and sleep. Inconveniently, my strategic plan had unintended consequences—namely, I had to start attending college classes. So I did. Strangely, the extreme cognitive dissonance of pursuing education at one of the most disadvantageous moments of my life failed to trouble me. Perhaps I had simply become too tired or overwhelmed to bother about coloring within the lines and just allowed myself to approach the world in whichever way worked best for me. Although this pursuit started off as no more than a need for personal hygiene, college suited me, and I was good at it. My desperation turned into excitement, and I was energized by the dialogue between the professors and students. In the midst of turmoil and confusion, I at last found things suddenly made sense, and my success grew from there.

During the brief car camping experience, I learned circumstance and money are priorities that are only as important as you allow them to be. Whether I was managing a poverty level or a multi-million dollar budget, the principles of both financial and personal management really never changed. I carry this lesson with me today as I progress through various leadership roles.

When the Japanese mend broken objects, they
aggrandize the damage
by filling the cracks with gold.
They believe that when something's
suffered damage and has a history
it becomes more beautiful.

~ **Barbara Bloom** (1951—)
American writer

Becoming Who I Want to Be

EVENTUALLY I GRADUATED with a bachelor's in
public administration. Since then, I also earned
two masters degrees and a Ph.D. in organizational
psychology. Today, although I am called Dr. T, I
still find myself amazed by my academic
achievements. More importantly, I am proud of
what they represent—namely, I am who I want to
be.

I now experience the world through my travels,
share my thoughts through the written word, and
have received awards and been recognized for my
efforts as a leader. I have had the privilege of
leading many individuals and teams through some
amazing feats. I strive to be a catalyst for women
to reach toward their personal and professional

dreams. Why? Because I relate to the struggles we all encounter. I have the desire to reach for the moon and stars, and I know options we have not thought of yet exist.

Over the years as I have reflected on those early school days, I discovered I am actually plenty smart, just not in the classic IQ-defined way. I regret allowing deprecating, albeit well-intentioned, advice to mold my opinion about my own capabilities. I choose not to be angry for those words spoken so many years ago, but rather am grateful for my understanding of how actions and words carry tremendous power. As a result, I routinely apply this insight with how I lead others—through guidance and respect—using the power of words to reinforce and inspire others.

There comes a time in the spiritual journey when you start making choices from a very different place. And if a choice lines up so that it supports truth, health, happiness, wisdom, and love, it's the right choice.

~ Angeles Arrien (1940—)
Cultural anthropologist

Money Matters

LEADERS MUST BE fiscally responsible. How ironic that the woman who once hated math eventually found herself responsible for a $50 million budget. You may be asking how that happened, and to be honest, I still ask myself the same thing! Did my math skills truly improve? Not really, but were they ever really quite so bad? To me, a more important shift was the way in which I viewed what the balance between leadership and fiscal responsibility meant.

Leadership is about creating an exciting movement through dialogue with people. Leaders act as catalysts by engaging people in the strategic direction, providing the necessary resources for work to be accomplished. It is about keeping people on the correct journey to allow the right work to get done, coupled with seeing the necessary course corrections and moving the team along that change. A great leader knows when to lead from the front and when to lead from behind. In other words, we need to let our people do their jobs and let them "get it done." Sometimes, we get in the way as leaders because ego blocks people from doing what they do best.

While a leader is providing sound strategic direction, she must always keep an eye on the financials. "Do not spend too much, do not spend

47

too little, or go over budget, and we will need to cut personnel"—those are the words corporate executives continue to shout from the top. However, it is my firm belief that fiscal responsibility is everyone's responsibility—and a leader needs to instill this in her people. It cannot be words shouted from the top; it needs to be an integral part of the daily activity.

Take, for example, a fulcrum scale—place leadership on one side and fiscal responsibility on the other. Each day, we must ensure we delicately balance the needs of our people, while constantly managing corporate resources. Sometimes one side of the scale needs to have more weight, and the next day—the other. Remember when you where younger and you were playing on the teeter-totter? Everything was great as long as each of you was in sync moving up and down. What happened when one person jumped off? Bam! This is what will happen to an organization if we do not balance leadership with fiscal responsibility: someone or something will come crashing down. Both people and money are important—treat them with equal respect.

The Plan is Bigger Than we Are

EACH DAY YOU wake up, remember life is a privilege. Open your arms and take in the breath of life. Know you are wise, believe you are strong, and appreciate who you are. Pursue whatever dreams you have, and sing the song you have in your heart. Align your passion with purpose, which can motivate you in a magnificent way. I fully subscribe to the thinking that one is better off teaching someone to swim than merely saving them once from drowning. Actively seek opportunities to learn from extraordinary women, and along the way, you may just discover you are that extraordinary mentor for someone else. Recognize where you may give someone a hand up in any way and be a part of the cascade of helping someone learn how to help others; you have accomplished the thing that is bigger than yourself.

Our Choices

WE MUST ACKNOWLEDGE and take responsibility for our failures *and* successes. Forgive those who could not initially discern you were a diamond in the rough. Reach deep down into your soul and decide your past is in the past. Focus on taking steps onto a new path—*your* path. Your journey may be bumpy, but choose to embrace and love those bumps because they are yours!

Words are powerful. They build and they destroy. Please think carefully whenever you choose to be negative. Even for adults, negative words can be internalized and have detrimental effects you cannot anticipate. I am not inventing a utopian world wherein no one ever gets negative feedback. I am merely suggesting you choose your words wisely and know a small Blue Jay reader—who needs your encouragement, not necessarily a husband—is inside all of us.

When you are wrong, suck up your ego and apologize. Ultimately, you will be regarded as having more strength and credibility than someone else who is never wrong. Don't be more concerned with being right than being happy. Women, more than men, are told we are not good enough in many different ways. Do not internalize this. Help other women; help the men as well.

Accept the misfit in you—own it and love it! Run your life the way you desire to run it. Remember, YOU are in charge of your future. Unless you have the courage to step outside of the status quo and try something unexpected, progress won't be made.

As a leader, you need to be the conduit for others to have the realization of the powerful roles they play. You are not convincing them to change, but rather, you are guiding them to discover their inner-core and how to be productive in the workforce. By the way, telling them to be what you want them to be is much easier; I urge you to refrain. Instead, guide them to their own greatness.

As a leader, you have a gift of words with an audience that is eager to listen. Build that relationship. Create the opportunity of synergy with people. Don't waste your energy on what they *can't* do and figure out what they *can* do.

> *You gain strength, courage, and confidence by every experience in which you really stop to look fear in the face. You are able to say to yourself, 'I have lived through this horror. I can take the next thing that comes along.' You must do the thing you think you cannot do.*

~ **Eleanor Roosevelt** (1884—1962)
First Lady of the United States

I constantly strive to view my life in new ways. My journey has taken me down many different roads, but all of the roads I traveled gave me the information I needed to create new possibilities. I offer you these leadership challenges. Please take a quiet moment and think through each one. My true desire for you is that these challenges free you to continue down your path of success.

Leadership Challenge

1) When was the last time you assumed something about someone else that wasn't true? What other explanations might be possible? And what types of assumptions have you made about yourself?

2) Without emotional and mental discipline, I would never have veered from the path I was following. What discipline needs more nurturing in your life?

3) My motto is "Change the world and enjoy life." What is your motto, and what are you doing to promote it on a regular basis?

4) Who played the role of your "loving" church member in your life? How do you ensure you never play this role in your business dealings with others who are counting on you for guidance and support?

5) Try to remember a time you felt like an outsider. What caused those feelings, and how was that situation resolved? Find a way to create an alternate scenario that turns being on the outside to your advantage.

NOTES:

Chapter 4

HELPING OTHERS GROW

by

Marlene Cain

Helping Others Grow

Just when the caterpillar thought the world was over, it became a butterfly.

~ Author Unknown

"You'll be sorr-rry,"♪ my best friend sang to me upon learning I was about to become a big sister. Both of us were age nine and "only" children when my friend gloomily predicted that life as I knew it was about to come to an end.

I remember silently resolving that I would *not* be sorry—that I would welcome the experience. Sure enough, after my baby sister was born, I did more than welcome her into our family; I loved taking care of her and watching her as she grew. The next year on New Year's Eve, my twin brothers were born. I was overjoyed that my status as a "lonely only" had forever changed, thanks to my three beautiful siblings. And just like that, we doubled our family size in 17 months—and tripled our diaper count!

Ok—maybe I was a *little* sorry about all those soiled diapers! We went through so many cloth diapers since this was before disposables that we didn't bother folding them; we just piled them somewhat neatly upon the changing table.

Taking care of my siblings at a very early age introduced me to the joy of *helping others,* especially important to my mother who became a single parent when my siblings were just four and five. As the oldest by 11 years, I was instantly promoted to junior Mom and took over many of the child-rearing responsibilities while our mother worked hard to support the entire family.

A Career is Born

IRONICALLY, IT WAS my childhood care-giving experience that prepared me well for biological motherhood, a career that never materialized, though I was destined to marry a wonderful man and am proud to say I have four children and nine grandchildren by marriage. My father's wry wedding-day toast was: "Yesterday you were single; today you're married, the mother of four, and the grandmother of one. How did this happen?"

Years later, after watching my family expand and mature, I experienced an epiphany while admiring my growing collection of miniature porcelain watering cans: Just as watering can help flowers grow, I liked helping *others* grow! At that moment, my life mission, fledgling company logo, slogan, and experience seemed to meld into the reason that I am here.

Be who you were meant to be,
and you will set the world on fire.

~ **St. Catherine of Siena** (1347 - 1380)
Patron Saint of Italy

The first time I realized I had discovered the work I was born to do was when I was an outplacement consultant with the largest transition management firm in the world. When a client company downsized, it would contact the firm and arrange for all types of assistance for displaced employees, as well as for those workers and management who remained. While attending an office function, I often expressed words of appreciation to management for having given me the opportunity to discover my life's work of helping others grow. Throughout the years, I consulted on behalf of this firm; I coached several thousand employees in skills that would last them a lifetime. Even though I was influencing the lives of others, I didn't consider myself a leader.

On paper, consulting with employees who had just been told they were being laid off doesn't sound like a fun assignment. But in practice, it was a whole different story. As I was coaching the participants in skills they would need in their transition to a new job or career, they taught *me* a lot about resilience, the human spirit, and the instinct to adapt, change, and survive.

I recall one particularly challenging participant who walked up to me during a break the first morning of a three-day workshop on career transitions. "Three days just to do a resume?" he grumbled. I politely responded that the workshop was actually much more than that and to please stay at least through the first day. He grudgingly agreed. At the end of the first day, that same gentleman came up to me and smiled, "Marlene, I don't think three days is going to be enough!"

Let the Entertrainment™ Begin!

MOTIVATING OTHERS TO make positive changes is a wonderful leadership attribute, but it can take some time. While attempting to change someone's mind can be *very* challenging, the possibility exists to influence someone's mind*set,* as in the case of our grumpy participant. And, I absolutely love that part of my career!

Humor has often been shown to be helpful in motivating others to make positive changes. Having an entertainment background with experience in stage, radio, television, and film greatly benefitted my seminars and workshops. One time so much laughter erupted in my workshop that the facilitators in the classroom next door rushed over to witness the merriment for themselves. That may have been the time a colleague dubbed me the "Entertrainer™." This was another one of those exciting moments when I heard a "click"—yes, that was *exactly* who I was— someone who enjoyed using her communication and entertainment skills to educate, inform, persuade, and motivate others to achieve their potential! Throughout these engagements, I derived the most satisfaction from being able to turn around situations that are perceived as negative into experiences perceived as positive and beneficial... in three days or less!

Leadership is like a lantern.
People gather around it and
see the world in a new light.

~ **Laibl Wolf** (1947—)
Dean, Spiritgrow Wholistic Centre, Australia

61

To me, leadership is guiding others and making a difference in everyday situations. And yet, I did not consider myself a leader, even though I was developing leadership qualities. As word spread about me, myriad companies began requesting I facilitate their workshops.

As I progressed in my career and the economy changed, I naturally shifted from consulting with organizations that were downsizing to companies that were "upsizing" and needed important staffing assistance. I stepped up to help dozens of premiere organizations hire hundreds of qualified employees.

In my downsizing days, I had noted that only employees who worked with large companies were being offered the benefit of a formal transition program. If an individual worker or small business wished to receive the same career counseling benefits, they were pretty much out of luck. So I decided to plug that gap and began offering individual clients and small businesses the same benefits their big brothers and sisters were getting from the large transition firms. Thus, Marcain Communication, an *Entertrainment™* consultancy focused on corporate staffing and individual coaching was an inspired founding.

In spite of all that I had accomplished thus far, I *still* did not consider myself a leader until a magazine editor asked me at a conference, "You know you're a leader, right?" Her question helped me realize that "Yes, maybe I *am* a leader!" I've observed that we women tend to downplay our leadership capabilities or simply don't recognize them. And yet, I believe leadership qualities such as risk taking, compassion, initiative, and stepping outside of one's comfort zone can be nurtured in all of us. If these leadership characteristics had not been nurtured in me, I am sure I would have walked away from my first theatrical audition, never hosted a cable talk show, not danced in a local Miss America pageant, ever launched a business, become a step-parent, or pulled up stakes and moved to a small town.

> *If you hear a voice within you say'*
> *you cannot paint,' then by all*
> *means paint, and that voice*
> *will be silenced.*

~ **Vincent Van Gogh** (1853—1890)
Painter

That Little Voice

MY MOTHER ADVISED us kids that one of the best ways to grow was to listen to "that little voice of truth within us." Wise counsel, but what can we do when we also recognize it as the voice of anxiety? Acknowledge it, and then act! I have learned that when I am considering a new venture and my little voice retorts, "What... are you *crazy?*" I know I am on the right track, and I don't back down. My drama coach reaffirmed that approach when he advised me to say, "Yes, I can do that!" and *then* figure out how.

About that time, I accepted a friend's invitation to accompany her and visit a Toastmaster's club meeting and wound up becoming a club officer of several clubs and later an area governor. I said yes to an invitation to become an ambassador for a Chamber of Commerce, later becoming a board member and subsequently elected Chairman of the Board.

What is *your* little voice telling you? Do you:

1) Attend a play and get that nagging feeling that you shouldn't be in the audience but should be up on the stage?

2) Find yourself saying, "Some day I'd like to do that?

3) Long for a career instead of a job?

64

4) Think you are too old or set in your ways to start something new.

5) Yearn to make a difference but lament "I'm only one person"?

Whatever your little voice may be saying to you, one thing is for sure, as Wayne Gretzky said, "One hundred percent of the shots you don't take don't go in." So what gives us the courage to take those shots?

1) A positive outlook.

2) A broader perspective.

3) A lack of fear.

With *just a slight adjustment* in each of these areas, you can lead yourself—and others—to ever greater heights.

A Positive Outlook

An exasperated boss once said to a cheerful employee, "Don't you have *any* problems?" Those of us in good moods tackle problems differently. We tend to move more quickly and reach solutions more easily, especially if we like to laugh. After watching a comedy in one study, 75% of the viewers were able to solve a problem, compared to only 13% of those who had not seen the comedy!

Certainly laughter and good moods can promote a positive outlook, but we live in challenging times. How can we maintain a positive attitude during the tough days?

A Broader Perspective

After suffering one of life's setbacks, instead of asking "Why me?" make *just a slight adjustment* to "Why is this happening to me *now*?" and "What am I supposed to learn from this?" Broadening our perspective can immediately lift a great burden, helping us move forward.

A Lack of Fear

Fear has a dual personality; it's nature's defense mechanism to keep us away from danger. But sometimes fear can become an offense mechanism, keeping us away from wonderful experiences.

When I was seven years old, I joined my friends at my favorite amusement park. They were having the time of their lives on a thrill ride aptly named the Whirlpool. After each ride, they called out to me, "Come on, Marlene; it's fun!" Four times I let fear prevail, but finally with their fifth shout-out, I was convinced to join them. My heart pounded as I entered the circular structure. I stood against the wall as instructed, clenched my fists, and tightly shut my eyes. The room began to revolve, slowly at first, then faster and faster. I opened my eyes just as the floor dropped six feet, but I remained flat against the wall! The force was with me... centrifugal force that is! From then on, the Whirlpool was my favorite ride, and I did it with my eyes open!

So I made just a slight adjustment. I decided I would ride all the "whirlpools" in my life. I also vowed I wouldn't let fear be the sole reason to keep me from attempting something I wanted to do.

> *The person who says it is impossible should not interrupt the one doing it.*
>
> ~ Japanese Proverb

You Are Someone!

LEADERS FREQUENTLY HEAR "We've always done it that way" or "It's never been done before" or "If there were a better way, *someone* would have thought of it."

Well, congratulations!

1) You are **someone**—a leader who will nurture a positive outlook and embrace a broader perspective, allowing those you lead to ride all the whirlpools in their lives.

2) You are **someone**—who will listen to her inner voice with confidence, lead with compassion, enjoy taking the initiative, and see the benefits associated with stepping outside of your comfort zone.

3) You are **someone**—who will inspire growth in herself and in others, and to whom no one could ever say: "You'll be sorr-rry"!

Leadership Challenge

TIME IS A finite currency. Even if you live to be 100, you'll only see the changing of the seasons 100 times. Each day, find ways to ensure you are making the most of the time you have for growth because you are exchanging a day of your life for it. This can be as simple as paying more attention to your "little voice" or making *just a slight adjustment.* Many believe your inner voice is your conscience, your soul, or the universe trying to communicate with you. It can save you time, offer a different perspective, answer a difficult question, or provide a new direction.

1) Can you think of three examples of how your inner voice has helped you grow?

2) Name one area where you could have a more positive outlook.

3) Select one area where you could broaden your perspective.

4) Take the next step in conquering a fear that is preventing you from a growth experience.

NOTES:

Chapter 5

LEADING OUT OF NECESSITY

by

Victoria E. Villalba

Leading Out of Necessity

Have the nerve to go into
unexplored territory.
Be brave enough to
live life creatively.

~ **Alan Alda** (1936 –)
American actor, director, and screenwriter

As a passionate entrepreneur and owner of a twenty-two-year-old successful staffing and recruitment firm, I provide highly qualified employees to fill interim, replacement, and new positions. In a nutshell, my company delivers peace of mind through career candidates who add value to a business. How did I get to where I am today? Twenty-two years ago, I was working for a national staffing company, managing a branch office in Miami, Florida. My career was going great, and I found fulfillment in my work. Things changed quickly, however, with one abrupt, unexpected phone call from our corporate office. The office I was working with had been sold and had become a franchise, which meant new leadership and a new direction.

The new owner, who I am grateful was a true gentleman and an honest man, shared open and honestly his plans for our team, and I, unfortunately, wasn't part of them. He explained, "I'm not going to be able to keep you longer than two or three months because I hope to do *your* job, once you train me." And with that bit of knowledge, I knew decisive strategic action was required immediately. My financial stability and professional development were at stake. Staying around for a couple of months to train someone, especially if I were going to be displaced, didn't make sense. With little hesitation I gave my two weeks' notice, determined to give my undivided attention to finding a new career.

In assessing my situation and all that I had learned in my short but comprehensive career, I knew two things: 1) my passion was recruiting, and 2) I was blessed with the skill for it, but where to turn? Which company merited my skills and abilities? For whom did I *want* to work? How would I protect myself from ever being in this situation again?

Royal Caribbean Cruise Lines was a client I had the honor of working with for some time and was most attached to. To be a true partner in the staffing world, you must know your client's culture and business. Its Human Resources team treated me as a colleague, and our partnership flourished in my two consecutive roles at different recruitment firms. This was where I wanted to work. When I asked if any work was available, I was told, "Sure, you can work as a contractor hiring our reservationists." I gladly did that for a few months and confirmed staffing and recruiting was in my blood. I had a burning desire to do this on my own. I was at a point where I'd been working long hours for someone else, and I thought, "How can I make this work for me?"

In the early part of 1992, I met with my mentor, the vice president of Human Resources at Royal Caribbean Cruise Lines, to ask for advice. "What do you think about me opening my own staffing company? Would you support me?" He said, "Sure, of course I would. You know our business, and you've served us well for years. We're very happy with you." This was music to my ears! Hearing praise from a client I admired and respected was extremely gratifying. This was the confirmation I needed—it was the boost of confidence that gave birth to my business.

Soon thereafter, I introduced a vendor-on-site model to Royal Caribbean. It wasn't an easy sell, even with a solid reputation and track record of success. In 1992, having a staffing company on location wasn't very common. In addition, trusting a small boutique company with such a hefty workload was a risk. It was a risk I am eternally grateful both Royal Caribbean and I willingly took.

My concept was born out of necessity. Since I was only twenty-seven years old, I didn't really have the resources or the credit to open up my own company with a brick-and-mortar office. My model would be about the service I provided, and I could save *them* money. It was a win-win scenario: I wouldn't have overhead, like phones or the Internet, or even computers; I'd be using utilizing all their equipment. The client would save expenses due to a low margin.

Today, the on-site vendor idea is very common. I can think of several national companies now on-site, but back then, I'm pretty sure I was the first staffing company to do this in the state of Florida. Also, I was trying to find a solution for this particular client. I knew from working with Royal Caribbean before that being very cost-conscious was extremely important to them. I knew if I could show the cost savings, they would probably go for the concept.

Trust your own instinct.
Your mistakes might as well be your own,
instead of someone else's.

~ **Billy Wilder** (1906—2002)
Film-maker

I ended up incorporating in March 1992. John Riley, vice president of Human Resources, went to the powers-that-be and said, "This is what Victoria wants to do, and she will save the company X amount of money. By doing this on-site, the staffing company will be right in the center of our HR department." Sure enough, that's how I began.

Inevitably, I needed to expand. Other former clients I had worked with would say, "Is that *your* recruiting?" when they saw ads I'd run, and I'd have to say, "Yes, but I'm only servicing Royal Caribbean because I'm on-site." In 1994, I opened up another office in South Florida, off-site. Things were moving really quickly.

At times, things got very tough. In 2001, employment began to take a dive because of the terrorist attacks. I had to downsize my operation by letting a few of our internal staff go, which was very painful. Then from 2007 to 2009, we had another economic downturn. I can't say my journey has been a cakewalk by any means. Business was slow, and on Fridays when I locked the doors, I would literally thank God we were at least still standing because so many other companies had gone under.

This journey has been the ride of my life, though—quite the adventure! I look at it like a roller coaster, where you have ups and downs and twists and turns. You hold on tight, that's for sure. Aside from the adrenaline rush, I really feel we provide a service; we find candidates careers. The ride is very exciting, and today, things are just booming. I've learned some important principles along the way I want to share with you.

Business Principles Worth Believing In

NEVER COMPROMISE YOUR **values.** This is the most important, whether you work for someone else, or your own company; never compromise your values. Period.

Be conscious of your spending. Business is a cycle. You have to be able to withstand the lean times. When business is slow, you have to tighten your belt. I'm very conservative, and I've never bitten off more than I could chew. I'm very lean in everything I do, in every decision I make. I purchase things and do not lease things. I make sure I own it. If things are rough, I know exactly what expenses I have. Keep an eye on your P&L.

Plan for the hard times. Without jobs, how can you diversify? What can you do? With my background in human resources, what could I do to generate income? I figured I could write job descriptions or create employee manuals for companies. Maybe I could do training, helping those who need help with resume writing? Be creative and versatile, and you will ride out hard times a little easier.

Build loyalty. I think over the course of the years, building relationships sustains you in difficult times. We've had very loyal clients. Even when things got tight, we were still their first call; the one company they would call for staffing. How can you create loyalty?

Be flexible. We have no choice but to change. I've learned so much from people who are younger, and this is also true of older employees. In 2011, my daughter graduated from college and came back to South Florida to join our company. This was a big change, not only for me, but for others, too. Having a creative person come in was wonderful. For example, technology is very different for my daughter than it is for me. She noticed how everything was outdated. Obviously, change can't happen overnight, but you can look for small steps to take today. My daughter became a partner in November of 2013.

Surround yourself with smart, talented people. I know what my weaknesses are, so I look for people who have strengths where I am weak. When I interview, I try to find somebody who *complements* me, who *isn't* like me. For example, I'm very serious and intense when I meet with a particular client, and I tend to get right into business. Having someone who works with me who is warm, bubbly, and can make small talk asking about the kids is exactly what I need. I'm very interested in all that as well, but it's just not my strength. Hire people who are not you.

Build communication skills. Communication means working with peers and dealing with clients. In today's market, we have many bilingual and even trilingual candidates, but unfortunately, they're not 100 percent in any one language. Can you write, read, and speak Spanish, or just speak Spanish? Can you speak business language or only slang? I'd rather have somebody who speaks, reads, and writes English perfectly than somebody who speaks three languages without proficiency in any of them. Each individual has the responsibility to develop his or her skills, not the employer. You want to be competitive.

Live in the present. I don't look back with regret, and I'm also not one to look to the future. I live each day, and say, "What are we doing presently?" What can we do better, not three years from now, and not on a five-year plan, but *today*?" I've seen a woman, who is the president of a large national company, in meetings with 300 people in the room. She is not talking, texting, or answering her email on her iPhone. When she speaks with you in a crowded room, she's not looking around. She makes eye contact *with* you. Have your heart and soul with everyone you meet.

Work hard. All our people, internally, as well as the people we place, have a very strong work ethic. We handpick the people who represent us. They are reliable and consistent. Our customers tell me that for an independent boutique-kind of staffing company, our image and brand is very different. What keeps us competitive is our work ethic. What is your competitive edge? Leverage it!

Get involved. We all know about joining professional organizations, but getting involved with nonprofits has been very rewarding, as well as good for my business. In a professional corporation, such as a human resource organization, several other staffing companies are members. Many of the nonprofits I've become engaged in really value how I bring my expertise in staffing and recruiting to them. What's most important is finding something you love and enjoy. In my case, I am involved with several foster care and adoption nonprofits because I'm adopted myself. I'm extremely responsible. I feel we should all give back to the communities in which we live, work, and play, but I've also been able to use this for growth, not just personally, but also professionally. What is your passion? Make time to get involved, and you will benefit both personally *and* professionally.

Seek mentors. Find not just one mentor, but several mentors in different areas. For example, I need help with work-life balance. I had an acquaintance who was a president of a local association. She worked full-time, had children, and was married, yet she seemed to have a balanced life. I asked her whether she could mentor me, and I never regretted my decision. Look to people in your professional and personal life whom you respect. Ask whether they are willing to give some time to mentor you; then pay attention! Their advice and counsel will be priceless.

Listen and learn. Being the leader of an organization can be lonely. Finding people you can trust and confide in, who might show you something new, who can be very honest with you and transparent, is paramount.

Twenty years from now, you will be more disappointed by the things that you didn't do than by the ones you did.
So throw off the bowlines,
sail away from the safe harbor,
catch the trade winds in your sails.

~ **Mark Twain** (1835—1910)
Author

Beyond Business

THE MIND IS a powerful thing. When we hear negative chatter, saying, "This won't work," or "I can't do that," we are setting ourselves up for failure. Some people are afraid to take a risk, but I like the challenge. We must replace the negative voice with a positive one in order to be productive.

I have a very strong faith, and I pray about things before I ever make a decision. I start my day, every day, in prayer. I pray for those people who might be coming into our office for an interview. When we have a belief system and positive energy, that's what really gives us the stamina to conquer obstacles. When we believe God truly has a purpose and a plan for our life, we realize how we still have unfinished business and much yet to conquer.

If you were to write your obituary, what would it say? Did you live your life exactly as you wanted? Did you follow your passion? If you don't come home at the end of the day with a sense of pride and fulfillment, make changes. If you are living out your passion and love what you do, you should sleep soundly and look forward to the next day. This certainly doesn't mean we won't struggle balancing work and home, but it should mean we are happy. May you find your happy place!

Leadership Challenge

Review the following questions and answer them honestly. Then apply the answers to your business and life!

1) How can you build and demonstrate a stronger work ethic?

2) What area could you improve to gain strong customer loyalty?

3) What weakness of yours could be overcome if you teamed up with someone with a different skill set?

4) If you were to seek a mentor, what might you wish to learn?

5) When are you *not* present in the moment? Who do you neglect or ignore, and how could you connect to strengthen that relationship?

6) How can being quiet build consensus? Do you allow others to debate ideas?

7) How much do you "own your brand"? How can you make your work more deeply personal and satisfying?

NOTES:

Chapter 6

CONFESSIONS OF A LEADERSHIP JUNKIE

by

Ann Marie Johnson

Confessions of a
Leadership Junkie

Leadership is much less about what you do,
and more about who you are.

~ **Jim Collins** (1958—)
Author of Hesselbein on Leadership

You would think I could easily find the time to cancel my gym membership, especially since the gym is within a mile of where I work. Visiting the gym was a priority I set for myself—a New Year's resolution. My husband provided me with a gift membership, and in the last year, I've walked in the doors three times. Somehow, I can't seem to find the fourth in me—and that for an administrative detail lasting five minutes. Why?

Good question. I am a strategic planner for a Fortune 10 company that pays me to think and solve problems, but I have noticed over the last few years that I can handle Corporate America's mergers and acquisitions better than my own life. I am no stranger to organization and prioritization as a married woman with two children in school who also achieved a master's degree and has twenty years of full-time work experience. I have the skill to manage a team of people and multi-million dollar projects. However, I seem to be too busy to find time to do little things for myself.

Throughout my life, I have attended all sorts of seminars on work-life balance. After several years, I finally learned that balance didn't mean giving half of my time to work and the other half to family. Balance doesn't equate to equal; it just needs to be fair. I try to be present and not multi-tasking. I understand what I should do, yet somehow in the equation, the "me" in life got lost.

The Dark Side of Leadership

LEADERSHIP HAS A dark side. From 8 a.m. to 6 p.m., I wear a suit. That navy-blue shield projects an image of competency. At the end of a business meeting, I am the first to volunteer for action items. At times, like everyone, I don't plan to take on more than I should, but others will suggest that I be on some team or project. The next thing I know, I am double and triple booked, and my life is out of balance... again. I know that I let this happen. The reason is simple: I like the feeling of being busy and validated. The truth is that I am a leadership junkie.

I supervise eight employees and serve on various teams. As a strategic planner, I work across the company and also with outside organizations. I have started spin-off businesses, as well as developed training classes. I mentor others. If something is broken, I fix it. If it's not broken, I might break it to see how it would work better! The financial rewards aren't what get me, although those exist. Pay is based on performance, and those with more output offer the perception of increased value. I have been promoted and bonused—they made offers I could not refuse. Over time, though, the money isn't what keeps me going—the please and thank you from team members is what jazzes me.

This doesn't just happen at work. I volunteer in the community as head of fundraising for little league and auction chair for the elementary school. I have served on four non-profit boards as a director. I delude myself that this is "for the children" and will directly benefit my own. Lies. *All* lies. When the benefit is done and I hear the event was the "most successful ever," I can't wait to top the effort the next year. The motivation is personal. I know that and can't help myself. I find that I am bored and restless if I am not booked completely on some committee or project. This isn't always fun; in fact, rarely is it. My stress level is quite high. I experience sleepless nights, have carpel tunnel, and gained fifteen pounds of weight as the direct result of eating from a vending machine. I suspect some of you reading my story can empathize with the thought that leadership isn't so much about the journey as it is the end result. We push ourselves, and the means aren't as important as the product. We are rewarded for our effort, more so if no one else is available to pick-up the slack.

Genius is one percent inspiration and ninety-nine percent perspiration.

~ **Thomas Edison** (1847—1931)
Inventor

Who wouldn't want to be a hero? When no one stepped up to chair the auction at the elementary school, I sat and waited for someone else on the Education Fund to volunteer. By the second meeting, the group of ten was lost without direction. I picked up a pen, walked to the flipchart, and started organizing things. By the end of the meeting, everyone was smiling or sighing in relief. I felt energized.

Leadership Opportunities

EXPERIENCE HAS TAUGHT me that leadership opportunities are found everywhere. Accidental leadership is not a new phenomenon but has become one to which I am addicted. I sniff out those opportunities. Right place, right time is almost as easy as wrong place, wrong time. For example, at work we might identify a problem, and I am the first to want to fix it, even if it's not important to getting my job done. I know I have the skills to organize and get results, and so I add one more project to my plate.

This has taken a toll on my personal life. Understanding that, I have tried to prioritize my family time and give to my husband and two boys as ferociously as I do with those I work with. On weekends, I unplug and drive to baseball and swimming practice, pay bills, do chores—none of these tasks are delegated to a housekeeper or nanny. I am proud to say that I have actually attended 90 percent of my son's baseball games, and scheduling conflicts tend to be family rather than work driven. What has been lost in the shuffle, however, is my sense of self. When I say personal toll, I mean personal in the deepest possible sense. I can't think of the last time I had a weekend to myself, let alone an hour to indulge in a hobby.

Somehow in all this living and leading, I lost track of the part of my family that takes the pictures and does the cooking and cleaning. My doctor had to bug me for three years to prioritize getting an overdue mammogram. And that's just the tip of the iceberg.

Leadership Lessons

DON'T LET THIS happen to you! Most of the stories in this book are likely inspirational. Feel empowered to grasp those opportunities for leadership and make a difference with what you are passionate about. But, learn two very important lessons from me: First, don't say yes to everything. Second, don't forget that only you can take care of yourself.

I labeled myself a leadership junkie because I can't seem to say no. The challenge of managing a team, the thrill of starting something new—I can't help myself. I used to think I took too much on because I was easily bored or wanted some sort of creative outlet. And then one day, I woke up at 3 a.m. and wondered why I couldn't sleep! Indeed, when was the last time I actually slept eight hours a night?

I had given so much and felt ready to snap. I cried. I had let my ego take me to this point. I heard all the advice about putting myself first and simply believed I was invincible. What price was I willing to pay to "have it all?" Must I do it all as well? I finally realized I am just as important as that capital project or that next fundraiser. My personal validation doesn't have to come from solving problems others either can't or won't. So, I am going to take that fourth trip to the gym. I put it on my calendar, like so many other things. Today, however, I won't postpone. I have the appropriate clothes for the occasion. What about tomorrow? Like any addict, I will probably need encouragement to break the habit and start new ones. I will be leveraging my network in a different way from now on. I might drag a friend along, but my husband is the one who bought me the gym membership, so I guess he will be coming, too.

Sometimes it's the smallest decisions
that can change your life forever.

~ Keri Russell (1976—)
Actor

You can take opportunities to celebrate success and reward yourself. I recently attended a luncheon for twenty years of service, only to find that those invited were to have a manicure and pedicure on company time. We weren't all women, which made it quite the diversity moment. Doing what's fun and what you enjoy can be a part of your leadership experience. Be creative and have a "walk and talk" meeting to build 10,000 steps and fitness into your day. Get out and smell the roses, literally, or huddle in a coffee shop over your favorite latte rather than sitting in a conference room.

We all have personal networks, and they are called personal for a reason. They are *yours.* Trust me, those people value you as an individual. So, set up a system that offers encouragement to work better, but also to balance life better. A random email asking how someone is doing can lead to a rich discussion. I'm not the only one who wakes up at 3 a.m. remembering what they need to do the next day. I bet I could text message one of my peers and find them awake worrying about their next deadline. When I started sharing how overwhelmed I felt, I heard "me too" from many others. A shoulder to lean on works both ways, so build your network into one that helps you succeed, professionally *and* emotionally.

The stronger and healthier you are as a person, the better a leader you will be. You may not believe this at first, but your peers will respect you for putting yourself first. I didn't think so until I saw it firsthand. When I said I couldn't take a trip due to a planned family event, I felt guilty. Surprisingly, my boss smiled and told me she was glad I let her know about the conflict. The meeting was rescheduled so I could attend, and the reason given was shared positively. I grew up in the corporate world where being the first to arrive and the last to leave was rewarded. Times have changed. Younger workers are challenging the status quo. Work-life balance is expected. Vacation carry-over is tracked as a negative metric. Don't be the last to say you can't check your blackberry during dinner. Set the example for those who work with you, and reap the benefits of reduced stress and improved productivity. I know you can do it!

Leadership Challenge

Let me challenge you! How will you view leadership of self as an opportunity? Will you schedule a long overdue doctor's appointment? Maybe you will sleep eight hours instead of five? Or you might ask for help from a friend. How can you take care of *you*? Because honestly, if you don't, then the 100 percent you give to others is for nothing. Love what you do, but love yourself just as much.

NOTES:

Chapter 7

BELIEVE AND WORK HARD TO ACHIEVE

by

Celeste Ducharme

Believe and Work Hard to Achieve

The future belongs to those who believe in the beauty of their dreams.

~ Eleanor Roosevelt *(1884 - 1962)*
First Lady of the United States

I grew up in Orange County and had two parents who loved and supported me exceedingly. With their love and support, I managed to make it through the normal numerous challenges most teenagers experience. Even though I lost my dad in my twenties and recognized it is never easy for anyone at any age to lose a parent, through life's myriad ups and downs, I always found a way to push forward with joy and succeed. Just how did I do this? I learned at a young age that to succeed I would need to separate myself from the criticizers and do-little's. Over the years, I have been fortunate to surround myself with respectful, committed, and hardworking, like-minded people who showed me the drive and desire to turn possibilities into realities.

We each have a person or event in life that guides our success. I built three successful businesses, but I realize that I am indebted to the foundation provided me by my mother, an amazing, loving woman. Always very close to family, I feel most fortunate about the relationship with my mother—who was much like a storybook character—loving, supportive, and encouraging. This love allowed me, even when I stumbled, to get back up and keep pushing forward.

The awareness of this quality of love was always with me; my mother was a stay-at-home mom. She was the mom who picked me up from school every day and took me to my sporting events; she was tennis coach, campfire leader, and softball manager. From a very young age, I felt the influence of that support and love, which allowed me, in middle school, to be acknowledged as both a scholar and top-performing athlete. In high school, I was honored as The Comanche Female Athlete of the year, and in 2000 was inducted into my high school Softball Hall of Fame.

I recently lost my grandmother. Perhaps I feel this loss so profoundly because she was the real foundation and strength in our family. I embrace just how blessed I was to have not just one, but two generations of strong, loving women influence who I have become. I must admit that it wasn't until I became a wife and mother that I started to appreciate and understand the sacrifices my mother made for so many years, and the hard work she put in—for me!

As a stay-at-home mom, my mother was not part of the traditional workforce, yet everything I learned from her helped me understand and integrate so many things into what ultimately became my leadership style. The experiences my mother passed on led back to my grandmother; we called her Jai Jai. Jai Jai was a single mom and business owner, at a time when it was uncommon. As I watched my grandmother manage an employment agency it was evident her position was not only an example to me; it was my training ground. I would go to the office and answer her phones and file documents, and learned at a very young age to complete each task professionally. Subsequently, during high school when my parents divorced, I watched how courageously my mom bounced back into the community and got a job. Not only did she begin working outside the home, but she became a spectacular business leader.

Mom stood tall and willingly took over my grandmother's employment agency. The examples of these two strong and loving ladies deeply imprinted in my heart and mind the power of women in business and leadership.

They instilled in me the need to be a self-starter, goal-oriented, and passionate. Most importantly, they taught me to lead by example, never to ask others to do something I wouldn't do, and to have a strong interest in encouraging others. The impact of being a self-starter was heightened when I became a wife and mother. I had to understand the importance of having goals and a scheduled "game plan" for each day in order to manage and deal with the responsibilities and organization of a unit larger than just myself. During that transition time, I was often reminded of going off to college where sports played an important part in my being a self-starter and working hard. I played volleyball, softball, and tennis. I practiced, worked hard at it, and as modeled by my mother and grandmother, laid a solid foundation of how to build success through hard work.

Unfortunately, because of an injury, my college softball career ended abruptly. I was forced to find a job and gratefully landed a retail position at Nordstrom. The leadership skills learned from my mother and Jai Jai served me well. I was with

Nordstrom just over three months before being offered a management position; another three months and the company promoted me again. Before long, I was positioned in buying, outside sales, and marketing.

When We Hasten to Believe

ONE UNDERLYING ELEMENT of success you will find is learning to believe in yourself and others. My strength lies in striving to be a godly woman and I feel so blessed to be a child of God! Philippians 4:13 states, "I can do all things through Christ who strengthens me"; Romans 8:28 promises "all things work together for good, for those who love the Lord, and are called according to His purpose." I suppose the verse that most touches my heart is 1 Corinthians 9:24: "Do you not know that in a race, all runners run, but only one gets the prize. Run in such a way to get the prize." These three scriptures created a strong, unshakable foundation of belief and success in my life, and I openly rely on them and share them over and over with those who come on my daily path.

Believing in others is an integral part of leadership. To look at, and embrace another person, and believe in their potential is a learned skill and one I am easily reminded of through raising two children. Through time, I loved and respected them unconditionally and strove to give them a role model to learn from and trust. My son, who will be graduating this May with his B.A. in Business, also grew up as a three-sport athlete. He graduated high school with honors and obtained a college football scholarship. My daughter, who is now 16, grew up playing softball, volleyball, and basketball. She carries a high GPA and has a love and passion for sports and life. Ten years ago when my daughter first showed an interest in sports, I stepped onto the field with her and became a coach and mentor to her and other young ladies. It was a conscious act to believe in and breathe confidence and encouragement into the young ladies.

What I did not expect was how much women need encouragement, no matter what age. I passionately believe this is truly missing in our society. Magic happens when you see skills and strengths in other women and call them out to "own it." The response is visible. This is particularly true in the teenage ladies I have been blessed to coach. I see doors open that make it possible to touch the lives of our youth. It is such a privilege to teach them lessons on the softball field they will be able to carry into life, their future careers, and family.

*Only YOU decide where you are going... goals
won't get you anywhere
—they will get you everywhere!*

~ **Dan Stephenson** (1943—)
Business advocate and humanitarian

Each Journey... a Path to Success

NOTHING GROUNDS YOU in possibility and success as does a roadmap to reach specific goals. It is so important to create monthly and yearly goals, look at them daily, and celebrate the success of the ones you have reached. It is sometimes necessary to redirect and recreate some goals you have, but I am a firm believer you must have a road map to follow. Along that path to success, you must surround yourself with other successful people—people who will inspire you through their own energy and connections with other successful people.

Along life's path, myriad possibilities present themselves as awareness, or some type of creative mindset, or a reaction to them. I believe the key is to acknowledge you want it and then go get it. I always say, "Believe and achieve." But, of course, hard work comes right along with that. If there is something you want, something you seek and desire, it **can** be yours. There is no "roof," nor an imagined limit in the sky to what we are capable.

107

The richest possibilities come from the heart and mind that opens you to the awareness of opportunities that you find the belief, courage and commitment to pursue. This is a God thing. He will firmly place His will and desires for your life on your heart, and then give you the drive and passion to attain these goals.

> *Your success and happiness lies in you.*
> *Resolve to keep happy, and your joy*
> *and you shall form an invincible host*
> *against difficulties.*

~ **Helen Keller** (1880—1968)
American author, political activist, and lecturer

Distinguishing a Leader

KNOWING THAT YOU have leadership skills requires that you address the characteristics you most embrace. For me it is 100 percent encouragement. In business, in my home, with my marriage, and with my children, my strongest characteristic is being the "encourager." Little doubt exists my leadership style was shaped by grandmother and mother, both of whom supported, loved, and constantly encouraged me.

I have often been asked whether a leader is born or made. I think a leader just needs opportunity. I had the opportunity to attend college. Although my injury impacted my softball scholarship, God opened a door for me at Nordstrom that ultimately led to a career that I loved. My mindset was not that I was never going to be successful or was somehow now a failure; it was, "What's next? Where do I move to now to continue the adventure?" Yes, we do experience tests and trials; however, as we push through, we reap the rewards and understand and grow from life's challenges and little "left turns."

I stepped into leadership in my first full-time management job at Nordstrom. The company had two rules: 1) The customer is always right and 2) If the customer isn't right, refer to Rule Number One. That made life simple: our goal was to please and take care of the customer. Over the years, I found that if I care for my employees in the same way, they will show me respect, effort, and support as well. This philosophy is extremely successful: to set standards and establish goals to help my employees push themselves to use skills they already have, but in which they may lack confidence. Over time I have successfully pulled the best from people and enhanced the many gifts they already have as I recognized potential in employees and players.

109

> *I've learned that people will forget*
> *what you said, people will forget*
> *what you did, but people will never forget how*
> *you made them feel.*

~ **Maya Angelou** (1928—2014)
American author, poet, dancer,
actress, and singer

Leadership Opportunity Demands Accountability

I HAVE BEEN with CK Self Storage for over a decade. In our weekly accountability meetings, the standard is to take feedback in all areas in addition to service and collections. I am grateful Nordstrom did not judge me by my age; it gave me an amazing opportunity at an early age based on my effort and attitude. As such, I am a fervent believer everybody deserves the same opportunity until proven otherwise. I give my managers the opportunity to lead with cooperative input as to what works and what doesn't. Together, we come up with solutions to their problems with realistic ways to address any issues that arise. This is possibly the most difficult part of leadership—delegating and letting others lead.

Leadership is a Natural Funnel for Coaching

LEADERSHIP IS A tool for helping people tap deep into the strengths within them. I have coached for ten years—all ages. It is a proven fact girls need to feel good about themselves in order to play well; I have had so many kids over the years come to me deflated—no longer able to believe in themselves. Girls need to be taught that success comes from effort and attitude. Skill will come with effort, and attitude will help them achieve.

Leadership Calls for Personal Reflection

IT IS NECESSARY to look back on situations and decisions to determine what you actually learned from yourself as you move toward being a leader of integrity. I take time every day for reflection. This reflection allows me to be proactive and see immediately how the words I say affect somebody. Just because we say something in a particular way, doesn't mean the message was received in that manner.

Leadership Calls for Implementing "Tools"

THE BEST TOOLS I have found include weekly follow-up and communications, asking, "What are the things that you were focused on this week? How did they go? How did your customers respond? How did your actions create results? Is it the direction you wanted to go?" Goals need to be defined and written. Reaching them requires creating attainable stepping-stones. Follow-up and communication about those steps creates a road map to help attain the results we hope for. This applies to business and on the softball field, at my office with my staff and with all of my players.

The purpose of life is to live it,
to taste experience to the utmost,
to reach out eagerly and without fear
for newer and richer experience.

~ **Eleanor Roosevelt** (1884 - 1962)
First Lady of the United States

Leadership Addresses the Deepest "Why"

WHEN I CONSIDER my deepest "why" I connect to the one thing that keeps me going when the

112

journey gets difficult... my passion to instill in others the awareness of, or the ability to have, a leading edge, by being prepared to do what other people will not. I send one definable message, "Stop making excuses, push through, and take control over what you have control over. Do not allow others to control your life. Keep going and push through." Each message is my way to reference 1 Corinthians 9:24—run the race to win; to receive the prize; to reach your goals—and in such a way that it can be respected and honored.

My ability to inspire runs deep, but it starts when I greet people with a smile. They feel my sincerity and integrity. It's important to me to walk a life of love and encouragement, not just talk it— and people sense what I say by the actions I take. It's not just talk.

Leadership equals encouragement, as people recognize strengths, work on weaknesses, and keep pushing through when life is not all they expect.

Life can be tough at times... and honesty and authenticity require I share my struggles. This sharing opens the door of communication with my players. I reflect back on my sophomore year of high school when my parents told me they were getting divorced. Many of the girls can relate to this. I share that I visited my high school friends in drug and alcohol rehab. It was hard for me, but I showed up to support and love them. And I am able to share not only struggles, but the success and power that comes from pushing through.

Marriage can be tough… it is not always easy and it takes commitment. I am so thankful that I ran in such a way to win the prize of a successful marriage. My husband is my true soul mate—it may sound corny, but after 23 years, I truly cannot imagine running this race without him by my side! When I am weary, he holds me up; when I am hungry, he feeds me; and when I am sad, he wipes my tears. My husband is also a very wonderful encouragement to, and the #1 fan of, my son, my daughter, and me. Pick a godly man, ladies!

Finances can be tough… people lose jobs, family, friends, or investments. In the self-storage business, when a customer comes in devastated over financial distress, I can relate because I've been there, and I didn't quit. I kept on going.

The loss of material things need not define who you are, no divorce defines who you become, and drugs and alcohol don't define who your parents are. It is the real life moments you share that demonstrate how you grew and pushed through. This gives others the confidence and the hope they can be whoever they want to be and can reach their goals. Seeing that I have come out stronger on the other side of struggles encourages both my employees and the ladies I coach. They see the hand of God is real and more powerful than any difficulty they are facing.

Leadership Perceives Criticism as Constructive

I HAVE A two-fold "belief system about criticism:"

1) **Q-tip**—which means to **quit taking it personally**. So what if it was a bad play or someone made an error right behind you; refuse to struggle—choose to quit taking it personally and get over it!

2) The second uses a **ladder**—get that ladder out and **get over yourself**. Get over the pity party, get over yourself, and get on with your life!

Yes, I am very bold, and it may be loving or harsh sometimes, especially with teenage girls. **I know** they're emotional and **they know** I mean what I say. They know I've been there, and they know I'm going to help get them to where they want to be.

Leadership is Celebrating Success and Being Quick to Praise.

I LEARNED A valuable lesson while at Nordstroms: to take quality time to write thank you cards and notes of encouragement. I transformed to a huge believer that you should put important, memorable things in writing and praise people verbally, which drives me to give notes and share small gift cards to celebrate goals reached.

Leadership: Making Difficult and Unpopular Decisions

WHEN WE MANAGE conflict, we help people accept change and be accountable for their actions. If there are obvious struggles in an employee's personal life, and it impacts work, I sit down and address it with them. Personal struggles cannot be ignored; they will not go away by simply ignoring them. I may, on occasion, have to carry a little more on my plate while someone goes through challenging times, or my manager may have to pick up the load. We all pick up the pieces for each other. You can feel it, and see how this level of combining accountability and support builds a team and a family.

Leadership Does Not Automatically Come with a Title

LEADERSHIP IS AN ongoing learning process. Being a "natural" leader requires a continual commitment to education and being around people who authentically share experiences of how they reached their success. But education is not sufficient without a support system. I feel blessed

I've had that while completing my college degree. My precious family sacrificed to allow me to complete my degree at night after working all day. Additionally, the prayers and encouragement of the businesswomen in the valley and my professional networking groups supported me.

Leadership Calls for Emotional Stability

A TRUE LEADER must manage her emotions, effort, and attitude. Choose to get up in the morning being joyful. My grandmother got up every day, and said, "Good morning, world. What great things do you have for me today?" She got up **expecting** great things. This mindset will contribute hugely to your success. Leaders also need to maintain emotional intelligence... it is the "right stuff" of effective leadership, and includes self-awareness, motivation, empathy, and social

117

skills. I choose not to let negative or critical people affect me. I use effort and attitude to take control of what I have control over... and then rest in knowing I've put my best foot forward and did the best I could. Leadership success is giving your very best effort with no regrets.

> *If you don't like something, change it.*
> *If you can't change it, change your*
> *attitude.*

~ **Maya Angelou** (1928—2014)
American author, poet, dancer,
actress, and singer

Leadership Challenge

Nothing happens without the convergence of passion and action. Create a "big" annual goal and list in detail the monthly goals you need to achieve it. Look at those goals on a daily basis, celebrate each success, and re-evaluate if necessary. To achieve those goals, surround yourself with successful, driven, passionate, and hardworking people who have accomplished goals similar to yours.

Leaving a legacy is to live in the hearts of the people around you, and leave a piece of yourself with them. This principle means everything to me. Looking back at Jai Jai's life and the lessons she shared has been invaluable to me. Watching my mother thrive both spiritually and professionally is a legacy I long for. Sharing these skills with my son, daughter, my employees, and the ladies I

coach is my heart's desire. Let effort and attitude direct your path. Believe it and achieve it! I believe in YOU!

NOTES:

_____

_____

_____

_____

_____

_____

Turn Possibilities into Realities

_____

_____

_____

_____

_____

_____

_____

_____

_____

_____

_____

Chapter 8

BREATHE THROUGH vs. MUSCLE THROUGH

by

Susan Kerby

Breathe Through
vs.
Muscle Through

The Heart and Soul of Leading With Grace

*Awake and be present to life...
ordinary people transforming the world with
our words; a world that works for everyone...
this shall be.*

~ Susan Kerby

I applaud your desire to dream.

As a leader committed to bringing forth new realities, you have a choice: "Do I want to muscle through or breathe through?"

Breathe: allow in, inhale, inspire, God-breath.
Muscle: force one's way, push, pull.

Both lead to results. Albeit, muscle tends to produce a promised and more "predictable" result and breath, I find, surprises us with desired and yet unexpected (maybe miraculous) results.

Both ways of being offer extremely different experiences on the journey. Muscle takes us up a path of struggle, upstream, effort, and force, while God-breath leads us along a magical path of surprise and delight.

When I see things I've wanted become real, things I felt sure I could never "make" happen, I call it enchanted play. My journey is about that process.

I am truly blessed; I'm living a dream come true. My husband Russ and I have been in business together for over 25 years. I'm the CEO and COO of his manufacturing company and Russ is the production manager of my "speaking biz." Literally, we have had each other's backs since we met when he managed my first seminar 25 years ago. We have a magical home on an acre of land in the hills of the Sonoma County wine country. It feels like a tree house where we look out over valley among the oaks.

But, let me reveal a bit more about myself. It hasn't always been this way! Most of my life I have been muscling to make the world go 'round. Pushing to get it to go my way. Always trying to control the uncontrollable.

And, for what? "To be liked?" Yup!

Being liked was my biggest dream. It seemed to be my default dream—not a lot of vision, but a lot of strategy to survive. I spent much of my life hiding behind my own superhero cape. I often acted "as if" I were powerful and popular, but I hid in plain view behind my Wonder Woman bravado.

In high school drama when told I was "acting," I said, "Yes, this **is** acting class..." I thought the class was where I got to be someone else. Confused, I didn't realize they wanted to feel me feel. One direct, yet accurate boy told me, "You are plastic, like a Barbie doll—nice house, but no one is home." What could a girl do? Nobody had taught me to feel or just be me.

I double majored in government and economics at Bowdoin College, an elite highly selective school in Brunswick, Maine. If you are from the East, you would be impressed, but to those from anywhere else... I was still able to hide in plain view. At Bowdoin, I set out to be noticed; I would hang and party with the best of them. Unfortunately, since I was rarely in the library, my dorm mates wondered how I earned good grades. Hiding behind the cape of "this is easy," I was bold—an extrovert. I pulled all-nighters to get my work done; no one would see me struggle!

My junior year, one of my roommates said, "You could talk to a wall."

Is that good or bad? It doesn't feel good, but I'll suck it up and smile and perhaps manage to laugh... as if it is funny.

It was important not to let anyone know I was hurting... that would make me vulnerable, weak, and unattractive. *Keep the plastic shield. Smile. Fake it 'til you make it. Muscle through it!*

No one else knew I was faking it—but I knew. Out of college, it was hard for me even to apply for jobs. I felt unprepared for what I would be asked to do. I ended up taking a job with Paine Webber in its Tax Shelter department. I didn't take it because it was a good job for me. *Strange choice, I typed labels to stick on envelopes when I had paid people in college to type my papers.* I took it because it would sound good to my college friends saying I worked at Paine Webber, but I was dying inside.

Five months later, I was introduced to transformational seminars.

Amazing! I see the possibility for learning distinctions that can actually help me in the present, in contrast to abstract readings of speculative utopias and hypothetical economic models.

When Leadership Calls

THE PEOPLE WHO invited me to step up and volunteer to provide leadership for these transformational seminars I figured were either desperate to fill their teams or saw me as more powerful than I saw myself. I decided to step into their view of me and once again donned my "bravado" to step into leadership.

Declare it and do what it takes to make it happen, at any cost.

And I did just that! By 1990, I rose to the top as a volunteer and began ten years of leading weekly seminars. It wasn't done with ease, and I wasn't very graceful, but I did produce results— and I did love facilitating the seminars that got others to "make things happen" for themselves.

One of my mentors told me, "Susan, you can **do** anything—the issue is who you are **being**." I told her, "This is the best being I got. I can't do any better being." Apparently "being" was a missing ingredient to creating results with grace.

Even as a seminar leader, I was in a constant struggle to be accepted by my peers. The same bravado and muscle-through attitude that helped me look successful by the results I produced, also pushed a lot of people away.

127

I kept doing more, hoping my drive to accomplish would help me fulfill my reason to exist and earn my right to be here. I remained invested in the idea that doing more of "making things happen" would get me liked.

I continued to put on the happy front, trying to look good in the process, but with all the effort to share the distinctions of transformation to make everyone else's life work, I failed at being happy in my own life.

I look like I have money, and it looks like I am happy—is this the best it will ever get? This isn't making me happy, but I don't know how it can be different.

In 2000, I was overweight and miserable; I found my business a constant struggle. I still tried to make the world go 'round by might. *I know how to make things happen—just get out of my way!*

The fake it 'til you make it path wasn't working for me. I just didn't know any other way. I could no longer tell other people "you can have anything you want in life when you participate in transformation," yet in my heart feel, "except for being thin and having money."

After 10 years, I stopped leading the seminars and turned away from the powerful, amazing models of authentic and effective leadership I couldn't seem to copy, and found my most transformational leader in the least likely of women.

Transformational Leaders

MY MOTHER-IN-LAW, one of the women I would have easily voted least likely to be a leader, is surprisingly the one who led me into being a leader with heart.

When confronted with the reality her thirty-seven-year-old daughter would die of Multiple Sclerosis (MS), and after Western medicine failed to help, my mother-in-law stepped out in faith; she went on pilgrimages to Lourdes and Medjugorje to ask the Virgin Mary for help.

When my mother-in-law finally returned from her pilgrimage to Medjugorje, she told me the Virgin Mary has appeared to some Croatian children on a daily basis since 1981. She was present with these visionaries during two of their apparitions and shared miracles she witnessed: the sun set twice in one evening, silver-chained rosaries became gold-chained, and people were struck with the Holy Spirit when prayed over by a priest.

I think, *Good for her! I am not moved. I am unimpressed by "second-hand miracles."*

I had come to think of God as a good bedtime story for those who needed something to believe in. My mother-in-law needed to believe. I was taught that I had me and that was all I needed. *I don't need God.*

Next, my father-in-law decided to go to Medjugorje and was determined to take some of his family with him; he offered to pay for his kids and their spouses to accompany him. I told my husband he should go; finally, I thought... *maybe I should go!* I wouldn't go to the North Pole looking for Santa, so I wasn't going to Bosnia looking for God. I decided I would just go as a tourist. When else would I get to go to Bosnia?

It turned out I was a tourist for only the first few days.

I can't deny what I feel and hear! I hear the voices of the visionaries who have grown up with daily visits from Mary, Queen of Peace. I hear God's voice. I feel the love of God. I am taught to listen for God's direction. I am taught to trust in God.

In Medjugorje, I slowed down enough, listened enough, and acted-as-a-pilgrim enough actually to feel! As we prayed, went to Mass, and talked to the visionaries, I found myself spending a lot of time contemplating the God I said did not exist. I began to feel the presence of divinity. I was told to turn things over to God and trust, and I asked in amazement, "You can do that?" I began to "try it out," a tiny little piece at a time.

Inspirational Leadership

IN APRIL 2002, I resigned myself to being 210 pounds and gaining an additional average of 10 pounds a year. What happened to my size 14 at my wedding 10 years earlier? Creeping up on a size 20, I was asked, "If this could be your best year yet, what would you want?"

I allowed myself a moment to dream and then declared, "I'll be a size 14 by Christmas and a size 12 by April, I'll pray and meditate daily, and I'll connect more with my friends."

Under my breath, I chortled, "Like that will ever happen!" I delighted at the ridiculous thought. It was out of my hands. I knew from past experience that no matter how much willpower I could muscle up, diets didn't really work.

Within a week, I discovered God intervening on my behalf. A business coach, of all people, was tired of my complaining and told me about a food program. She said, "It's really rigorous and I don't think you'll do it, but if you did it, it would work."

How dare she! Oh, yeah? Watch this!

She knew just what to say to get me to prove her wrong. I was scared to dive in, but I was more scared not to.

Oh my God! All my prayers for "my best year yet" were answered at once. The food program also required that each day I pray, meditate, and reach out to three friends in our program to talk about what was really going on. It was everything that I'd asked for, and yet, nothing I wanted to do. Although it felt uncomfortable, it felt right and I knew I had to dig in.

My friends watched me and demanded "What are you doing? I want in." And as naturally and effortlessly as breathing, I began to draw 'em in. In short order, not only was I connecting once or twice a week to the exact friends I imagined when I declared that I wanted to connect more with my friends, but I was being a messenger of hope. My presence was a physical billboard demonstrating that seemingly impossible dreams can become reality. God is good. I could not have even dreamt up this solution.

Oh, yes, I was a size 10 by Christmas and am still a size 10 more than 13 years later!

Miraculous Leadership

IN 2010, I was called to return to Medjugorje. Blessed with many miracles over the last ten years since Mary first called me to Medjugorje, I mused while praying a rosary, "What did you bring me for this time, Mary?" and I heard, "I brought you to introduce you to my Son, Jesus." I didn't expect any response; certainly not that one.

On the tour of town, we were told to go to the Adoration Chapel to ask Christ why he brought us. In silence I replied, "OK, Mary, I'll go."

I knelt down and demanded of Christ, "Why am I always so defensive?" I heard, "Please don't be your first line of defense. You be vulnerable; I'll keep you safe. You can be both vulnerable and safe." Then I heard something about being "humble and grateful" and I cried and then sang, "Jesus, remember me, when you come into your kingdom." He interrupted my singing, "Susie, remember me, and you'll come into my kingdom."

Wow! My mother-in-law led my father-in-law, who led me to Mary, who led me to Christ... who led me to trust and be vulnerable.

Recognize When it is Your Time

OVER THE YEARS, many have followed me as I became a leader with grace. The journey is never without effort, but it can be miraculously easy. My own story is one of my big dreams... of making money by speaking and leading transformational seminars. In my ten years as a volunteer, I led over 300 transformational seminars, in front of 15,000 people. I was passionate and I loved the mission, but there came a time both to make a difference and make money from my speaking. It was my time.

Every quarter I *declared* my target income from "my speaking biz," but in reality, most months speaking income was under $100. On a hunt I kept wondering, *Who will pay **me** to train for their company?* I kept talking about my speaking biz... **my** speaking biz... One day finally, "I got it!" My speaking biz—my speaking biz—God was directing me to train people to speak. **That** was my "**speaking** biz."

*Not only can I make a difference with **my** speaking, but I have been given a mission to help God's messengers and help them do so in an outstanding way.*

Today I get to "Change the World One Speaker at a Time," transforming speakers *on a mission* who make it their business to get their messages out. Their messages transform from awkward to awe-inspiring. Nothing makes me happier than carving away everything that's in the way of authentic expression and natural resonance to have audiences drawn in saying... "I want what you have."

When God Speaks... Listen!

I'VE BEEN TALKING about writing a book since 2000 after my first "pilgrimage" to Medjugorje (the one where I was a self-proclaimed rosary-praying tourist).

I even have a title for it: *God Believes in Us: I Was Called by a God I Said Did Not Exist.* I imagine myself going on speaking tours. I feel called to pass along Mary's simple message for the nonbeliever that changed my life: "Spend five minutes a day contemplating the God you say doesn't exist and God will do the rest."

Earlier this year, I dared to risk. I said yes to what scared me and didn't seem to make sense. In a talent show of speakers exposing their hidden talents, I read a story I had written and shared with my parish on Good Friday: *I am Thirsty.* I called my "act" "Susan Kerby Unplugged." For one who loves a good adrenaline rush of being on stage and being outrageous and engaging, I went out of my comfort zone and sat on a stool, barefoot in my jeans and T-shirt and read directly from my script. I felt vulnerable, yet I trusted; the audience leaned in and listened. Several people thanked me for bringing them back to God from that talk.

Wow! Humbled and grateful, I'm amazed that from a willingness to expose what is most meaningful to me, I received an invitation to speak all the way across the country, a year from now, as the keynote inspirational faith speaker for a special, prayerful group of women who come together to renew their relationship with the Lord. Oh, yes, and I was invited to be an author in this book!

Once again, breathing in the grace that always surrounds us, my dream is finally becoming real. No longer do I seek to muscle my way through life... grace walks hand in hand with enchanted play.

God Called Me to Leadership

ONCE I THOUGHT, *I am but a shining star cloaked in the darkness of fear and self-doubt.* Waiting to step out, waiting to shine, and waiting for permission... for what, I don't know. It feels like I was waiting for marching orders—to be told exactly where to go and what to do. We are trained to be patient, do as we are told, and wait for someone else to lead us out.

The qualities of a leader include courage, boldness, humility, and gratitude. As women, we are being called to step up and lead with faith, heart, trust, and compassion.

Stop waiting; this is your time and you have permission to rise up. Be bold. Courage isn't the absence of fear; it's the presence of faith.

Enchanted Play - Turn it Over to God and Trust

TURNING POSSIBILITIES INTO realities is delightful when you learn to breathe through versus muscle through; it comes when you are open to lead with grace. "Turn it over to God and trust!"

Dear God, turning possibility into realities begins with a prayer. I often didn't even know I was praying, but I realize now how many of my private hopes and dreams have been heard and answered. When I listen and follow Your lead, You confirm I don't have to muscle my way through life... When I breathe, and lead with grace, I experience joy the way You meant life to be... through enchanted play.

When asked, "What is your system for turning possibilities into realities?" I reviewed my journey in meditation. In the quiet, God revealed my seven-steps for "enchanted play" :

137

1) **Dream.** God likes you to dream big. There is no degree of difficulty in miracles.

2) **Declare**. Share what you really desire. Be specific. God listens, no matter what you believe.

3) **Delight**. Turn it over to God and Trust. When dreams feel too big for us to manage, we lighten up. (This step is the difference between muscling through and breathing through.) Laugh. Wonder. Expect miracles. Chortle as you tell God, "Can't wait to see how you get this to turn out."

4) **Discover**. Watch and see. Be a detective. Pay attention to what you say or hear over and over again. The Universe is telling you something.

5) **Dive in**. Give it a try. Say yes, especially if it scares you. It could cost you your aliveness if you don't risk.

6) **Dig in.** Keep going. When it feels right, even if it looks wrong, trust and have faith.

7) **Draw 'em in**. Bring another with you. Reach out and grab a hand.

Leadership Challenge

I challenge you to declare a dream and follow it through the seven steps of enchanted play. Delight in the unfolding. It need not be a difficult path!

"It's impossible,"

said Pride.

"It's risky,"

said Experience.

"It's pointless,"

said Reason.

"Give it a try,"

whispered the Heart!

~ Author Unknown

NOTES:

Chapter 9

LAUNCHPAD FOR SUCCESS

by

Guylaine Saint Juste

Launchpad for Success

And like air, still I rise.

~ **Maya Angelou** (1928—2014)
American author, poet, dancer, actress, and singer

I was 28 years old when I decided to end my first marriage, and separate from my daughters' father. At an age when my friends pursued graduate degrees, thought about marriage, and contemplated their futures, I found myself faced with a divorce, responsible for two children (one of them with a life-threatening condition), the owner of a home on which I owed more than its worth, and saddled with a sizable amount of personal debt. I could no longer stand to live feeling stifled and used.

Though he said he loved me, I had come to believe that my husband tolerated the state of affairs because he convinced himself of his lack of options. I couldn't allow the fear and anger that paralyzed his heart to handcuff me into staying. I was too enthralled by the force pulling me forward, like that of a quicksand, to think about my future or possible consequences. I suppose that's how people who abandon a house on fire might behave... self-preservation propels them simply to get out—with little or no regard for what is left behind.

Leaving my marriage actually represented a subconscious attempt at leaving my very self. I loathed and despised the woman who looked back at me in the mirror, and the man who had introduced my adolescence to love, commitment and responsibility. The scepter of promises and dreams he held was shattered beyond repair. I rushed out of that life with the irreverence of brokenness, too oblivious to worry about tomorrow, pushing toward a new identity.

When Life Launches...

DECEMBER OF THAT year strolled right in and washed upon my new shores the remains of holidays passed. My daughters were seven and two and our two-bedroom apartment, where they, my mother, and I lived, felt oddly unfamiliar to them. It also did little to shelter them from their father's relentless and unyielding anger. And yet, there was nowhere else for me to run and hide.

Sensing my despair the closer Christmas approached, my mother coerced me to take some time alone. That afternoon, I left with the best intention of seeing a lighthearted movie that would enliven my mood with some holiday cheer. Yet, as soon as I pulled away from the house, I heard a screeching sound. It was deep, tense, and had the tenor of a discorded accordion. Not until the salt of my tears reached my lips did I become aware that racking sobs and rushing tears had been released from long being held hostage. All that had happened in the past six months came crashing in, and I pray never again to experience the darkness of that moment.

The deafening silence of the car forced me to turn on the radio for relief, and Cindy Lauper soulfully sang to me that she could see my true colors. And there, in the confines on my car, I learned that God speaks to us by different means, and that...

1) my past doesn't define my present...

2) in His eyes I am enough and beautiful... and

3) I am crafted reverently to be a witness of grace and love to the world.

It was too much to take in at that moment; however, I knew in that instant that "goodness and mercy" would follow me and on their laps I would find the strength, wisdom, and resilience to carve a new path: *Taking a position of family leadership, I was finally confident we had landed on the Launchpad to Success.* I had been handed a bottle of Windex and a soft cloth to scrub the windows of my soul and allow the light within to shine forth.

Leading the Way to a New Future

If you find a path with no obstacles, it probably doesn't lead anywhere.

~ **Frank A. Clark** (1860—1936)
American politician

THE NINE YEARS that followed were knitted with laughter and tears, heartbreaks and new friends, job loss and promotions, stances and staccatos, drum rolls and violins, deep losses and subtle victories, and always the unerring, unwavering presence of my God's love, about which C.S. Lewis writes: "Love is not affectionate feeling, but a steady wish for the loved person's ultimate good as far as it can be obtained."

Less than three years into my new life chapter, I lost my mother unexpectedly. We were never good friends. She wasn't an affectionate woman, and I clearly kept coming short of her ideals. Yet, she always stood by me, and saw me through my darkest days. I didn't know how to be in this world without her, and her granddaughters were at a lost in her absence. Now, we were really alone... the three of us.

The day my mother died, my resilience was put to the test. She waited for me to arrive at her bedside. I think she wanted to know I didn't feel abandoned because she was moving on. Oh, the grace of having had the opportunity to reassure her! I climbed into her bed and told her that the entirety of her life had been all about her only child. I spoke of the pain my father inflicted when he left when I was just six years old, and reminded her that sickle cell disease and the constant crises, which rocked her small frame, had no life in heaven. I made her look deep into the tunnel to see her own mother and brother waving her on. And on that last day with my mother, I thanked her... for her courage, her fierce independence, her refusal to call it quits, and for out-living the statistics. I held her hand as she released her soul, and wiped away the oxygen mask that covered her face.

As I lay there alone in the hospice room, tears failed to come. Their absence persisted when I picked up her urn and flew to Haiti where I laid her to rest. A reservoir of toughness availed itself during that time, its corset held the frame and structure of life in place. In retrospect, the very act of stepping into a position of family leadership was a natural segue into a life of "leadership." Those lasting moments with my mother impacted how I moved through the next leg of my life journey—leading my own children to their future.

I believe my mother met Saint Peter at the pearly gates and promptly demanded an audience with The Almighty. Within weeks of her arrival in the hereafter, things began to change, and imperceptible shifts began to take shape. As if gathered by our sorrow, my girls and I organized as an inseparable triangle whose angles were welded into each other. They stopped agonizing over the cancelled promised paternal visits, learned to rely on each other, and got involved in playing basketball. Despite my eldest having sickle cell disease, she would go on to play varsity sports at a top high school.

We bought our next home in exactly the neighborhood my mom and I had visited not long before; it was the perfect definition of a fixer upper. Yet, a contractor waltzed into our life just to beautify it at cost. Other pieces of the puzzle fell into place at work, and in three years I earned two promotions, which positioned me for middle management at the bank where I worked. I also noticed a shift in how my position as family leader became easier with the advantages offered through my expanding career, and how sometimes the family leadership seemed more successful when I embraced our fun, connected moments.

The numbers in my paychecks began to allow for disposable income and the girls benefited from my indulgences. The weekly "family night" ritual on Fridays involved dragging their mattresses to my bedroom and filling it with Chinese food or pizza smells. We took short vacations, traveled for basketball tournaments, and ice cream cones at Baskin Robbins® found their way back into our diet.

Leaning into Life's Lessons

I PRESSED ON in life, ever more challenged... always pushing, stretching, and affirming the lessons life sought to teach. We lived in Fairfax, Virginia and my job required that I travel 40 miles one way, every day. The girls attended a private school that did little to demonstrate the faith it pretended to instill in its pupils. The brutal traffic from Montgomery County to Fairfax meant that I was often late to pick them up, and mercilessly, the school imposed fines for late pick-up on an already expensive tuition and after hour care fees. Soon that unyielding pressure convinced me to move the girls to public schools where they were given access to tools and resources to excel. That also meant the girls became underage "latch key" kids.

I am eternally grateful for the neighbors who either turned a blind eye to the obvious and to those who stepped in to help. Laura often had to knock on the door and walk my youngest to school when an early meeting had me out the door at the crack of dawn. I owe Laura a debt of gratitude for keeping my then six-year-old in the security of her home when after school activities prevented my twelve-year-old to welcome her home.

Life got harder when my older daughter was recruited to a private high school 35 miles away from our home. We had to leave by 6:30 a.m. to make the car pool ride and that meant leaving my seven-year-old alone for at least 90 minutes. That choice also entailed my older daughter taking the metro from school by herself at 13. There were many times when the traffic caused me to arrive late to pick her up at the metro station.

I still remember her meeting me at the curb of the metro line, all bundled up against the cold, praying she would escape a sickle cell crisis. There were also grueling basketball practices that ended at 9 p.m.! My youngest hated them, for it meant leaving the house at least 70 minutes early to pick up her sister. Summers offered no respite; camps and basketball tournaments filled every available moment. Between work and my girls... there was no time left for me.

I heard of a Chinese lesson where a pupil asks his master, "How does one endure?" To which the master replies, "You endure by keeping on enduring." So we kept on—the three of us—until I met my husband in 2007, and married him in 2008. It took patience and resilience to organize our new life and embrace a new set of lessons!

Reflections on a Journey Well Traveled

Without deep reflection one knows from daily life that one exists for other people.

~ **Albert Einstein** (1879—1955)
German-born theoretical physicist
and philosopher of science.

AS I REFLECT today, every turn of the journey brought me closer to the good life I now enjoy. First, the Bible proclaims, "Your enemy will become your footstool." I understand this to mean that adversity forces us to rise and to grow, and often the very person we think is an enemy serves as our greatest teacher. Be respectful to those who hurt you most as they allow you the greatest opportunity: to meet ugliness with grace, and conquer pain with gratitude and thankfulness.

My greatest failures served as the launching pad for my best successes. Nothing makes you change course and readjust the way mistakes do. The key is to learn from the thoughts, actions, and behaviors that fueled the undesired outcome. The swifter... the better!

My favorite movie is *Finding Nemo*. I love the scene where Nemo's father is swallowed by the whale. He is panicked and afraid... until he is out of breath and comes to realize the whale had covered thousands of miles bringing him closer to his destination. I, too, have been swallowed by the whale! People, events, and situations I thought were against me have often turned out to be my greatest catalysts.

My daughters and I often played the "what if" game. We earnestly questioned our paradigms. That game came in handy following my mother's death: *What if when we die we are really born and when we come to this world we die to our limitlessness?* It was important to me that I model grieving and healthy mourning for the girls. We cried together, shared memories, and used the "what if" game to find hope and allow faith to conquer fear.

In her poem "Still I Rise," Maya Angelou's words echo in my consciousness: "Up from a past that's rooted in pain, I rise. You may cut me with your words... Still like air I'll rise." In a metaphorical valley, I packed my bag for the climb to the mountaintop. I believe in the strength and resilience that live in me, and their power to see me through.

Reaping the Rewards of Family Leadership

To the highest leadership among women it is given to hold steadily in one hand the sacred vessels that hold the ancient sanctities of life, and in the other a flaming torch to light the way for oncoming generations.

~ **Anna Garlin Spencer** (1851—1931)
American educator, feminist, and
Unitarian minister

IN MAY 2013, my first child graduated from college: Presidents Leadership Program honoree, Distinction in Service Award, and Dean's List. The night before her graduation, as we were having dinner, she reminded me a time long ago I had promised her to wear a St. John suit to her graduation. That promise was made to encourage her, after one of her classmates in middle school dubbed her "arrogant" for sharing her dreams of going to college. That child felt my daughter should have said, "**If** I go to college," instead of, "**When** I go to college."

When I made that promise, the thought of spending several thousand dollars on clothes was farfetched at best. That night, my child said, "You forgot, didn't you? Or perhaps you thought I forgot?" I was brought to tears. In February of that same year, I happened to stroll into a high end store, fell in love with a St. John suit, and after a little persuading from my husband, decided to splurge, fixing this luxurious indulgence to the impending special May date. I had totally forgotten my promise, though it was obvious my daughter had not. I cannot find the right words to describe the look on my daughter's face when I told her, "Promise made, promise kept." She welled up with pride.

My daughter walked up on stage, and when they called her name, and began to read her many accomplishments, I am the first to admit I came undone. I stood on a chair, with arms raised... tears streaming down my face, shouting her name over and over again, laughing and screaming while I was rocked by a conundrum of emotions, which

154

included: satisfaction, extreme joy, contentment, excitement, thankfulness, gratitude, and yes, I humbly admit, a pinch of pride!

One of my greatest victories rests in the moment after her graduation. There, in front of everyone, my daughter lovingly presented me with a plaque. In those precious moments when she thanked everyone for coming to celebrate with her, she said, "I dedicate this moment to my mother without whom this wouldn't be possible. My mom has been my sister's and my rock; our inspiration. I am who I am today because of my mother." My breathless reply, "You are a dream come true, beloved child. You and your sister gave me a reason to get up when I didn't want to. This is a dream come true."

As of this writing, my youngest child has committed to play basketball in college and will spread the wings to her future come next fall. Another part of my dream is in the making. My babies, now both adults, are highly contributing, conscientious, responsible, and accountable members of society. Yet they remain silly, playful, carefree, and kind, making a good impression on people who meet them and... I have the enviable position to be their mom!

I never got to hear my mother tell me that she is proud of me, although I ask her often where she is now. I still don't have an answer to that question; all she says is, "Press on; keep pressing on." So I work to prepare for the next chapter of my life. I am not sure how life will be without basketball games, sports tournaments, homework, projects, and the raising of children. Yet, I exhale and take stock and am comforted thinking... *Not too shabby for a young woman who arrived in the U.S. from Haiti at the eve of her eighteenth birthday, barely speaking English, going to college while raising a family and working full-time.*

I know there is more to the story, and still I rise!

Lessons Develop Characteristics

THE LESSONS I learned raising my children shaped the leadership values I seek to live and exude:

Leadership Characteristic #1: First, the Bible proclaims, "... your enemy will become your footstool." I have always understand this to mean that adversity forces us to rise, to grow, and that the very person we think as an enemy serves as your greatest teacher. I encourage peers, people who report to me, partners, and bosses to challenge my thinking openly. I refuse to submit to the imperialism of corporate hierarchy. Even when it hurts, I have come to realize that I have grown much as a leader, a woman, and a human because of those who opposed me.

Leadership characteristic #2: Own your mistakes and admit to them. I believe people will follow leaders who are humble, honest, and have the ability to say: "That was a mistake; I am sorry; how do we learn from this and do better?" I also allow people the space to do the same and not attempt to hide or lie. The number one responsibility of a leader resides in creating an environment where people can be their best selves and contribute greatly in ways that inspire them and bring forth their passions.

Leadership characteristic #3: The best gift I have received from an employee was a kaleidoscope. Jason told me he'd come to realize I see the world as through a kaleidoscope; his gift singlehandedly allowed me to find my voice as a leader. Life projects in hues of colors and shapes... interconnected, despite the twists and turns. As with television and movies, leaders are called to shed the black and white reels and bring forth excellence in others. Applying an "Ask don't tell" philosophy, I have found, creates cohesion of thoughts, ideas, processes, and truths that ultimately move a team and an organization from diversity to integration. Ultimately, excellence is not good enough. To win in business and in life, we must be willing to engage, connect, and integrate to set and reset standards.

Leadership characteristic #4: Own your story and who you are. The suggestion isn't to spread your personal life around. Rather, it suggests that you allow people a peek—a glance—into the story that has shaped you. I believe the more human a leader is, the more people connect with them and allow themselves to be vulnerable and humble. Seeking perfection seems wasted energy in my book. I prefer to lead where my best self resonates.

> *Imperfection is beauty, madness is genius and it's better to be absolutely ridiculous than absolutely boring.*

~ **Marilyn Monroe** (1926—1962)
American actress, model, and singer

Leadership Challenge

Own your story and own your voice. What does it look like—sound like? I am not talking about the bland words on your resume. Do people know what you are about and does that engage others to connect, collaborate, and buy into your vision?

158

NOTES:

Chapter 10

FROM FEAR TO FAITH

by

Lisa Marie Platske

From Fear to Faith

I dwell in possibility.

~ **Emily Dickinson** (1830—1886)
Author

My fairy tale story below parallels my life, living as if "Someday" was one of the seven days of the week. The delays I caused took me out of the world of wonder and possibility and down the slippery slope of doubt and fear. Fortunately, like most fairy tales, my story has a happy ending.

Once upon a time,
in a land not too far away,
in a time not too long ago,
there lived a brilliant woman.
A talented woman,
who imagined a wonderful life
as a difference maker…
But instead of taking action,
she would daydream about "someday."
She was creative at making excuses;
She was the queen of "looking busy."

She was paralyzed by the fear of
"getting it wrong,"
or worse… failing.
She promised herself "Someday. . ."
She was going to write a book;
She was going to exercise again;
She was going to travel the world;
She was going to make her mark;
She was going to live an extraordinary life.
Then one day,
that brilliant and talented woman realized
those things won't happen, not now—
not ever—
unless she stopped making excuses;
unless she stopped being afraid;
unless she started taking action.
It was at that moment
she wrapped her arms around the idea that
she could choose "Someday!"
She could move in the direction of "Someday;"
She could commit to Someday being right now
and start taking action—
because it's not too late
to turn possibility into realities.

~ Lisa Marie Platske
2014

CHILDREN COME OUT of their mother's womb
with their minds a blank slate waiting to be filled
with information. Nobel award-winning scientist,
Daniel Kahneman, speaks about how you

experience 20,000 individual moments each day, and most of them don't leave a trace and are completely ignored. However, the mind takes in experiences and learns to fear or be fearless—to doubt or trust—to sit and wait or leap and risk.

Shaped by countless individual moments from my childhood, I waffled back and forth from feeling completely inadequate to feeling powerful beyond measure and believing I could do *anything* I set my mind to doing.

I grew up in the 1970s in a blue-collar town in Pennsylvania. My father left my mother, my sister, and me for another woman when I was only six years old. To this day, I remember the trauma and disconnect as I didn't understand what had happened to my idyllic family life. Anyone who doesn't believe kids have deep thoughts and profound awareness of their lives and circumstances is clueless. I was keenly aware of how differently I was being raised by a strong, single mom who did her best every day to hold our family together. The world certainly didn't make things easy on her. Divorce was something people whispered about in conversations back then, as if they were talking about something dirty. Some of the parents in the neighborhood wouldn't allow their kids to play with us because we came from a "divorced household," not home, but household. Oh, how I just wanted to fit in and be like everyone else! Every day I faced the fact that I was different from all of the other kids in my small Catholic school because of this one life circumstance, albeit a big one.

I spent my childhood being shuttled back and forth across town, between my home and my grandparents' place as my mom did her best to provide a stable and loving environment for my sister and me. She signed us up for Girl Scouts and enrolled my sister in sports, always volunteering so she could encourage and reinforce we could be anything we set our minds on. I saw the daily struggles, and as I sat in my Catholic school desk, I was pretty sure the God of Heaven and Earth the nuns talked about wasn't concerned about my small life, and I was confident He reserved His love for "other people." And, by other people, I meant rich people.

My favorite pastime was to play with Barbie dolls in the basement of my grandparents' house. Ken never had much of a role in my Barbie adventures—no romantic get-a-ways or weddings to fantasize about. In my Barbie story, Barbie did everything herself. Despite my grandparents' strong influence, I was the product of a single-parent household and was keenly aware you shouldn't rely on a man to be there for you—ever.

Not Too Long Ago

EXPERTS HAVE FOUND the frequency of small, positive acts matter and negative emotions can lead to serious problems in the mind and body, including stress and anger. The magic ratio is to have five positive interactions for every one negative experience.

In the classroom, I found a way to get consistent positive reinforcement. While I was not the "cool" kid (looking back at how awkward and socially inept I was), I excelled in my studies. I triumphed when I saw an "A" in red by my name on the top right-hand corner of my tests and felt validated and worthy. By the time 8th grade rolled around, four students, including myself, had gone through the textbooks for 8th *and* 9th grade. Yes, we had the same book in high school, and the teachers didn't know what to do with us. The school bought a trailer and hired a special teacher to work with us. Mandatory reading included Norman Vincent Peale's *The Power of Positive Thinking.* Homework included writing phrases from the book on 3x5 index cards and carrying them around, memorizing Mr. Peale's wisdom. When the instructor filled up a glass and asked us to describe what we saw, I remember writing down mostly negative words. I couldn't see half-full when my world felt half-empty. I recall reading "out of every adversity comes an equal or greater opportunity" and thinking, "He doesn't have a clue about what's going on in my life!"

However, I wanted to believe in unlimited possibilities, and I wanted to believe anything was possible for me. So, I bounced back and forth from faith to fear, fear to faith.

> *"Above all, be careful what you think because your thoughts control your life."*

Proverbs 4:23 (ERV)

Webster's Dictionary defines trust as "the firm belief in the truth, ability, or strength of someone or something." Since thoughts of unworthiness ran my life, trusting in something—anything at all—was challenging. When my grandfather passed away, I lost my one positive male role model. Along with him, my desire to have a relationship with God died, too. I felt God needed to prove how much He loved me, and so far, He wasn't doing such a good job so I would just rely on the trinity of me, myself, and I… if I couldn't count on God. Slowly but surely, I began doing that with *all* my relationships, proving that I was strong and secure and didn't need anyone. I could do life on my own.

By relying solely on myself, I found even when I was in a relationship, I was lonely. My life was about muscling through each task so I could prove I was good enough.

- ✓ Go to college. Check.
- ✓ Date good-looking men. Check.
- ✓ Get a degree. Check.
- ✓ Date more good-looking men. Check.
- ✓ Get a great job that pays well. Check.
- ✓ Date even more good-looking men. Check.
- ✓ Get promoted. Check.
- ✓ Date still more good-looking men. Check

I never stopped to think, "Can I do this?" I just pushed my way through the fear and the "what ifs" to show the world I was worthy of being alive. I was hard on the outside, and a hot mess on the inside.

In one of my many relationships, I dated a man who encouraged me to start attending Mass with him. One week at Sunday Mass, I read a blurb about a SEARCH retreat in the church bulletin. I had never been on a retreat (actually they seemed a bit too "holy-roller" for me), but I felt it was a sign as it fell on the 5th anniversary of my grandfather's passing.

"For know the plans I have for you,"
declares the Lord, "plans to prosper you, ...
plans to give you hope and a future."

Jeremiah 29:11 (NIV)

That weekend, I began my life anew. How many times had I thought: "I'm not good enough? My past was too ugly? I've made a mess of my life? How could anyone love me? On that weekend, I laid my burdens down and gave myself permission to be open to giving and receiving love fully.

My journey to being able to turn possibilities into realities comes with a faith component, something I don't often speak about. While I'm not here to preach to you, I would be inauthentic if I didn't share what actually happened to me to enable me to stand in my own strength and power and have the courage to bridge the gap from a what if to a what is.

When I think about what happened, I realize that this was the first step to opening my heart enough to risk failing. Before, I tried so hard to impress people with how smart I was. I wasted energy on worrying about getting it right and not being good enough to the point where I wasn't any fun to be around. And, at times, I was a bit of an Eeyore, still seeing the glass half-empty. What I learned was every single day, we must carry out acts of trust with our family, friends, coworkers, and strangers in the world. In order to exist, we must rely on others. We do not live alone. Because humans aren't perfect, there are times when the people I trust are going to get it wrong and hurt me. Making this choice is much more liberating than hiding out for fear of being hurt and missing out on something great in life.

A Wonderful Life

IN WORKING WITH my coaching clients, I talk about building a wellness center that encompasses all seven areas of our life: physical, emotional, intellectual, spiritual, financial, relational, and work/creativity. When one area is out of balance, it's like dragging a trunk of junk everywhere we go. Nothing seems easy.

After the retreat, I continued growing in all aspects. I acknowledged I still had a lot to learn and was willing to improve. Realizing I had made peace in all areas except that of romantic relationships, I made a list of the fifty-four things I wanted in a man. While my friends scoffed at the idea, I believed I was deserving of a lifetime love and that meant getting clear about what I wanted.

Up to this point, everything I did to turn a possibility into a reality was internal or centered around my own choices, but this was different. Amazingly, I discovered that like everything else I had achieved and accomplished, loving myself was critical to inviting the love affair of a lifetime into existence. I had stopped waiting for my prince to show up on my doorstep and decided to be active and write down what he looked like and trust he was out there. I cannot express this enough. Clarity serves as the first step in getting what you want.

Jim and I met on the job at a train-the-trainer conference when we were both working in federal law enforcement. Over dinner, I discovered Jim was Catholic but not practicing. He shared how he stopped attending Mass because his life was good, and he didn't see what going to Mass would do for him. I explained how participating in the Mass isn't all about getting. As a community of believers, we bring our individual gifts and talents to the faith community on Sunday. When someone is absent, everyone suffers because we all bring different gifts to the church community. Our time together ended, 9/11 happened, and we weren't brought together again for another nine months while we were mentoring sister classes at the Federal Law Enforcement Training Center. Once again, life took its twists and turns and several months passed before we went out on our first date. By now, I was doing my best in my life to hold on loosely, enjoy the ride, and trust that everything was happening for a reason. I'm proud to say that when I left my job in the government, I had transformed who I was and earned the nickname of Mary F'in Sunshine (Thank you, Gloria).

172

*Whether or not it's clear to you,
no doubt the universe is
unfolding as it should.*

~ **Max Ehrman** (1872—1945)
American writer, poet and attorney

On one of our first dates, I brought up my list of fifty-four qualities to Jim and explained that in order for me to enter into a relationship, he would need to live out his faith actively, or else we'd simply be good friends. Jim rekindled his faith commitment, and after a year and a half long-distance relationship, he proposed in the St. Patrick's Cathedral in New York City right before the evening Mass.

Trusting the Journey

I CONTINUED SPENDING time being versus doing, taking the time to listen, pray, and trust so I could be present in the wonder of today. One of the biggest opportunities to turn a possibility into a reality was after our wedding. Three thousand miles from home, with no family or friends living nearby, I set out to open a leadership training and development company. Clearly, my passion for leadership would give me the lifestyle I wanted so

I could invest in my marriage; I took a risk and embarked on a journey like no other. Could I turn this possibility into a reality? Equipped with my faith, a strong belief in myself, and a loving husband to back me when I doubted my ability, the answer was a resounding "YES!"

It is not the mountain we conquer, but ourselves.

~ **Sir Edmund Hillary** (1919—2008)
New Zealander mountaineer and explorer

Looking back, I realize if I had given it a lot of thought, I would have gone back into law enforcement. After all, what did I know about business? I had a criminal justice degree and a master's in Human Resources. What did I know about leadership? Yes, I was a supervisor in the government, but I only made it to mid-level management. Who was I to teach and train? I was young and had a limited range of experience in the world. And, don't let me get started on the "what ifs" that popped into my head: "What if no one hires you? What if people think what you're teaching stinks? What if you fail?"

I was back to finding the glass half-empty. Why didn't I see my brilliance? Why didn't I think, "What if so many people hire me I can't handle it?" Or "What if people love me that I'm overwhelmed by the requests for work?" "What if I succeed?"

174

These are all part of the same big lie that plagued me many years ago. Fortunately, I had learned a few lessons along the way. Check in with God. Know who you are, who you're not, and what you want. Start with a written plan. Trust that everything is happening for your highest good. Connect with people who want to see you succeed.

Love yourself every step of the journey. I didn't have a clue whether I was doing it "right" or not, but I just kept putting one foot in front of the other, taking one action at a time, and trusting every step on the journey.

> *"The journey of 1,000 miles starts with one single step."*
>
> ~ **Lao Tzu** (604 BC – 531 BC)
> Chinese philosopher and poet

Design Your Destiny

IN TEACHING MY clients the deep importance of designing their destinies to live a life centered on their values, I challenge them to create action items next to each area of the seven areas of well-being. To model what I teach, I utilize the same process for myself.

In 2010, in the area of spiritual well-being, I committed to going on another retreat. After my first epiphany, I can't say I was expecting much. What I discovered was not only a deepening of my faith but the realization that in my busy-ness, I had slowly started to rely entirely on me. Reverting back to my past "be in control" and "find a way to make it work," I had stopped listening and breathing. I got back to basics and began getting amazing results for my clients.

Fast forward, three years later, and I was stuck again. I noticed something wasn't working. Instead of taking action, I earned a degree in making excuses and looking busy. Sure I had clients who were getting results, but something inside me was paralyzed. Someday had become another day in my life again.

I share this so you understand that choosing to turn a possibility into a reality has taken more than willpower and might. It starts with choice, then direction before moving into commitment and consistent action.

If you can dream it, you can do it.

~ **Walt Disney** (1901—1966)
Creative genius/entrepreneur

My lesson of accepting each day as it comes to me and not wasting time or energy on wishing for different circumstances isn't easy. I struggle with trusting, even though I pray for strength and guidance throughout every work day. I'll admit that years ago, I was angry about what I perceived as my crummy little life. I thought "rich people," aka people who had more money than me, were happier. I've realized how far off base I was.

I wear different hats in my business: speaker, trainer, coach, advisor, and mentor. But the hats I wear most proudly are those of lover of life, difference-maker, loving wife, daughter, sister, and friend.

Today, my office has signs everywhere that echo the ease with which I turn a possibility into a reality. My mom gave me several of them: "Don't try so hard to fit in when you were born to stand out" and "...If you have faith as small as a mustard seed, ...Nothing will be impossible for you." (Matthew 17:20, NIV). Jim reinforces every day by leaving me notes, tucked in my suitcase when I'm traveling, or on the kitchen counter when I'm in town. The ones on my desk are: "Proceed as if success is inevitable." "You are worth more than you know. Capable of more than you think." "Yes, YOU can do it!" "Infinite possibility... live your dream," and "You are amazing."

Grateful for my fairy tale life, I sometimes stop and pinch myself at how it's all evolved. So, how do you turn a possibility into a reality? Well, that's simple. It's all about taking the journey from fear to faith. The world is full of possibility. If you can dream it, you *can* do it.

> *You may have a fresh start any moment you choose, for this thing that we call "failure" is not the falling down, but the staying down.*

~ **Mary Pickford** (1892—1979)
Canadian actress, co-founder of United Artists

Every day when you wake up, you have the opportunity to choose what you want and the direction you will take to get there. I believe leadership unlocks the door to countless treasures. Leadership guru John Maxwell says, "Leadership is influence, nothing more and nothing less." The greater the influence you have, the bigger your impact in the world—and the wider your sphere needs to be in order to create an impact that makes a difference in your family, the community, and the world—one person at a time.

Sometimes the only
available transportation
is a leap of faith.

~ **Margaret Shepherd**
American writer

For the past twenty years, I have researched leadership and its effects on people. The bigger the risk, the bigger the opportunity. I've opened myself wide in making myself vulnerable and sharing personal parts of my story that some of my closest friends have never heard. Women lead differently because they see the world through a different lens—one of creating collaborative partnerships, which is why I wrote my third book, *Connection: The New Currency,* with 12 other co-authors. If you don't know how to connect, you cannot lead. Every so often, I attempt at flying solo, and the end result is always to crash and burn.

Kouzes' and Posner's research found the top four characteristics people want in a leader are: integrity, forward-thinking, ability to inspire, and competence. I would add to the list that leaders must also be vulnerable and transparent. My leadership style has changed greatly, recognizing that great leaders ask great questions because it's not about them; it's about the people *around* them. The question I ask most often is, "Am I someone worth following?"

Here's what you can do to be someone who easily turns their own possibility into a reality and step in to your own leadership. First, start with a written plan. Take the time to write down what you want. (Remember the list of the fifty-four qualities I wanted in a man?) Even if it seems silly, the act of writing down what you want on a piece of paper tells every cell in your body that you are serious about what you want.

Second, spend more time getting to know who you are. The more self-aware you are of how you operate, the easier it will be to implement your plan. For example, I am a big-picture strategist who has learned to embrace the details. Details, processes, and systems are important, but I am conscious and aware that my brain does not naturally think about them first. Instead, it builds the big picture. If you are someone who values details and struggles to create a big vision, then develop your plan by working backwards, outlining everything you know you want.

Thirdly, build partnerships. As you've heard throughout my story, no one goes it alone. You need support. We all do. Partnerships can be formed in many different ways and do not have to be formal agreements. When you have a written plan and know who you are, knowing who would be a great asset in your life and how you can add value to someone else's world is much easier. With these three elements—your plan, your personality, and your partnerships—you'll be on your way. And the world needs your brilliance.

Leadership Challenge

I believe the secret to life is knowing what you want and being willing to ask for it—moving from fear to faith. Usually, we only ask for what we think is possible. Experts may challenge us to set "stretch goals." My challenge to you is about you digging deeper. About what are you paralyzed by fear right now in your life? And, what is one action you will commit to taking so that you can make a bigger difference in the world?

NOTES:

Conclusion

MAKING A DIFFERENCE

*It is a funny thing about life; if you refuse to
accept anything but the best,
you very often get it.*

~ **W. Somerset Maugham** (1874–1965)
English writer

ASKING THE QUESTION, "How do I get where I
am to where I want to be?" happens for most of us
every day. While it may not be a conscious
question, I believe leaders seek to continually
learn, grow, and develop throughout their lives.
Yet, this growth can be encumbered by everyday
life responsibilities and challenges. I've often
looked at others and wondered how they get so
much done and have had others ask me the same
question. We each have our own bandwidth for

what can possibly be accomplished in 24 hours, but this cannot be an excuse for moving forward. For if we ever stop asking the questions, that challenge us to bridge the gap from "what if" to "what is," our ability to use our gifts and serve the world in the biggest way possible stops, too.

On April 9, 2013, Forbes magazine shared the definition of leadership as a "process of social influence, which maximizes the efforts of others, toward the achievement of a goal." In authentic leadership, when one person wins, everyone wins. If you've gotten this far in the book, you've read through (and hopefully taken action on) the Leadership Challenges from these top experts. I trust they have moved you further along on your own journey. As I've said before, the world needs your brilliance!

Whenever Jim and I travel, we book our hotel and flights but very little else. Wanting an authentically local experience, we spend time wandering around the city watching the people and taking in the energy of our new surroundings. We sit in the park, a café, or the subway station, sharing stories about what we're both experiencing. However, all of our travel is not random, as we do visit the attractions that are unique to a given locale, and they require some advance planning. Most of our travels have been to places where English is not the native language, and since English is the only language we are both fluent in, it makes our encounters all the more exciting.

One afternoon, we were heading to Parque del Oeste to see Templo de Debod, an ancient Egyptian temple built in 200 BC and relocated to Madrid, Spain in 1968. Our hotel was on the other side of town, and we took the subway there. Because Jim and I don't plan every detail, we trust we're going to get to our destination on time. We got off the subway and looked at our map, which wasn't a very good one, and had difficulty discerning which direction we should head. After several minutes, we agreed the temple must be across the street at the top of the hill.

We crossed the street and began our trek. About half way up the hill, something just didn't feel right, and so I stopped a woman who was walking down the hill. In my broken Spanish, I asked her for directions for Templo de Debod. She smiled and pointed down the hill! Then, she shared it was right behind where we were standing looking at our map. This meant we were right where we were supposed to be and went in the *opposite* direction. Fortunately, we were only three minutes off course and could easily turn around and head back in the right direction.

185

This experience relates to our everyday lives. How easy it is for us to get off track, even with a map and pretty good sense of direction. When we stop, however, and ask for help, we can find ourselves back on track. This book is designed to encourage you and remind you to do just that. And, don't forget to trust your instinct!

We do not have to become heroes overnight. Just a step at a time, meeting each thing that comes up, seeing it is not as dreadful as it appeared, discovering we have the strength to stare it down.

~ Eleanor Roosevelt (1884–1962)
U.N. diplomat, humanitarian, U.S. first lady

When you're someone who has chosen to take the road less traveled and seeks to turn an idea into a reality, you may think the energy and enthusiasm you have for what you're working toward is enough. It's not. Brilliant minds recognize how stopping to evaluate if you're heading in the right direction and asking for assistance along the journey will get you to your destination faster. Imagine if Jim and I had continued our course without stopping and asking for directions that afternoon. While I'm sure we would have eventually arrived at the temple, our journey would have taken some twists and turns

186

that would have delayed us getting to our next stop on our itinerary. And, even though I always trust and enjoy the experience, I'm not so short-sighted to go blindly without a map and directions when I want to arrive at a destination. Life is a journey; be as prepared as you can with the proper tools and good maps.

For The Greatest Good

I AM THE type of person who is always looking for ways to simplify my life, which is why I like to create acronyms to help me remember important things, in addition to this being part of my Federal government training. One of my favorites reminds me how I'm the one who is ultimately responsible for the outcome, the results, and the ability to turn that possibility into a reality. I call it: "AALL about ME." Let me explain. This doesn't mean I don't need anyone. In fact, it's just the opposite. AALL about ME stands for: Ask - Assess - Listen - Learn - Make Changes - Evaluate. By asking the right questions, assessing a situation, actively listening, being open enough to learn what's being shared (I find this one to be the most challenging and used to dare someone to teach me something new), choosing what changes would work for you, and evaluating whether you're moving in a better direction or not, you rely on others for their help and support. Hopefully, you now know we are all

187

here to support you through the pages of this book.

Whether transitioning from a thought or an idea into something that is tangible and real seems daunting or doable, the actionable steps it takes to be in motion are simple. Simple doesn't mean easy, though. What amazes me when I listen to other people's stories of triumph is how they each have the same elements in them. Reading each of the chapters, I've been inspired again and again for my own journey. I've also shed a few tears along the way—not tears of sadness but of hope and joy, for without these women, the world would be a very different place.

What we do in life, echoes in eternity.

~ Maximus Decimus Meridias
Roman general, from the film "Gladiator" (2000)

Ultimately, when we choose to step up and give a voice to our big vision, we speak up for those who are struggling to find theirs. Our choices in our life echo throughout the halls of the world giving people permission to stand up and speak their own truth. And, this is the real power behind top experts bridging the gap between a possibility and a reality. Resources

Author Biographies

*We must believe that we are gifted for
something, and that this thing,
at whatever cost, must be attained.*

~ **Marie Curie** (1867—1934)
French physicist and chemist
Two-time Nobel Prize winner

THE WOMEN WHO so generously contributed to
Turn Possibilities into Realities have shared their
insight, wisdom, stories, and strategies about
stepping into a place of leadership. They've given
advice on how to look at life's possibilities and
step into a position of power when the opportunity
presents itself. Their individual perspectives
enhance the power contained throughout the
pages of this book.

What you may have already noticed, which is
different about this book, is the contributors'
varying backgrounds, ages, and interests. The
women who are featured and who courageously
share their stories come from incredibly diverse
environments, educational experiences, and skill
sets. They are educators, CEO's, entrepreneurs,
non-profit leaders, mothers, sisters, daughters and
wives. Their experiences include working for

enterprises ranging from Fortune 500 companies, to being solo entrepreneurs. The components that bind them—they have all embraced leadership and give freely of their time, talents and abilities, without expecting anything in return... hoping to make a difference in the world.

> *There is no passion to be found*
> *playing small—in settling for a life*
> *that is less than the one*
> *you are capable of living.*

~ **Nelson Mandela** (1918—2013)
South African statesman

Lisa Marie Platske

From Fear to Faith

Lisa Marie Platske left her action-packed life as a Federal law-enforcement officer to become CEO of an international leadership training and consulting company, Upside Thinking, Inc.

An award-winning leadership expert, Lisa Marie creates effective leaders. She takes her law enforcement journey, which began on the piers of New York and ended post 9/11, and shares with you what exceptional leaders do differently, why connection is the new currency, and how to position yourself strategically for big opportunities.

A certified master coach, Lisa Marie has worked with multi-million dollar entrepreneurs, non-profit leaders, and start-ups from three continents and in 20+ different industries, on how to position themselves as an expert in their fields. Her proven success strategies have resulted in her clients getting six-figure opportunities, tripling their income, securing bonuses and promotions, and finding up to 21 extra hours in each work week.

The author of *Designing Your Destiny and Connection: The New Currency*, Lisa Marie lives in Alexandria, Virginia with her loving and supportive husband, Jim.

Educational Background

M.A., Human Resources Training and Development
  Seton Hall University, South Orange, NJ
B.S., Criminal Justice,
  University of Scranton, Scranton, PA

Major Accomplishments/Recognition

Women in Business Champion of the Year
  Small Business Administration (SBA), 2010
President's Call to Service Lifetime Award
  George W. Bush, 2008
Woman of the Year Award
  For You Network, 2008
Woman of Excellence Award – Rising Star
  National Association Female Executives (NAFE), 2007

Contact Information

Contact Information
Upside Thinking, Inc.
(951) 334-9162

LisaMarie@UpsideThinking.com
www.UpsideThinking.com
www.LeadershipSuccessSummit.com

Dr. Theresa Ashby

Just be You!

Theresa Ashby, PhD, MBA is founder and CEO of Ashby Business Consultants, LLC.

After faithfully serving as the Vice President for a large healthcare organization, she knew it was time to expand her reach in order to dedicate herself to re-imagining corporate success through the way people interact.

Theresa, by nature a strategist, advisor, and thought partner, seeks to empower leaders to create, enrich, and accelerate their organizations to greatness. As a consultant, she partners to leverage the capabilities of the organization by energizing people and helping develop relationships. Through her speaking, she passes along her knowledge and experiences, sharing lessons both from successes and disappointments, ultimately inspiring audiences to perform at their best.

Theresa is a lifelong learner who has enjoyed extensive international travel, learning about different cultures, studying business practices, and engaging in rewarding philanthropic work.

Educational Background

Ph.D., Organizational Psychology
  California School of Professional Psychology,
  Los Angeles,
  MBA Business
  University of Redlands, Redlands
B.S., Public Administration
  University of Laverne, Laverne

Major Accomplishments/Recognition

Outstanding Women Award 2014
  Women's Leadership Summit
Whitehead Leadership Society
  University of Redlands
Inductee to Leadership and Academic Excellence
     2013
  School of Business Society
Senate Appointment 2012—2016
  California Earthquake Authority Advisory Panel
Business Press 2010
  Exceptional Women Business Leaders of Inland Empire
Nomination: Best research paper for China cohort.
  Ashby, T. (2013). Guānxi. International Marketplace:
  Perspectives from Asia.
University of Redlands, study abroad course.
  Ashby, T. (2012). Secrets to a Successful Project: Let's
  build a few hospitals.

Contact Information

Ashby Business Consultants, LLC
3943 Irvine Blvd. #617
Irvine, CA 92602 (949) 533-8832

Theresa@AshbyBusinessConsultants.com
www.AshbyBusinessConsultants.com

Garet Bedrosian

Leadership from the Inside Out

Garet Bedrosian believes in human potential. Her life mission is to understand the ways we come to know ourselves through the relationships we form with one another. She has learned our minds and bodies are inextricably linked, and healing requires we address both.Garet is an author and speaker with thirty years of experience leading groups, consulting, and facilitating workshops. She holds several certifications in IMAGO relationship therapy and is an accomplished workshop presenter for couples and individuals.

She enjoys facilitating Equus workshops with groups because of the transformational nature of the experience. A local and international Bioenergetic trainer, Garet is also a certified Bioenergetic Therapist (a somatic psychotherapy). She is the Executive Director of the Southern California Institute for Bioenergetic Analysis and also serves on the Board of Directors.

Educational Background

Masters in Social Work,
  San Diego State University, 1983;
  Concentration in mental health; Master's Essay: "Blended Family Problems in a Social Context"

196

Bachelor of Arts, Sociology/Psychology,
  University of Arizona, 1980. Graduated cum laude
A.C.S.W., 1993, Academy of Certified Social Workers
Certified Bioenergetic Therapist (CBT)
  Imago Relationship Therapist
Workshop Presenter
  Certified "Getting the Love You Want," "Keeping the Love
  You Find" and "Recovering Our Connection"
Certified Expressive Therapist (CET)
Certified Level 2 EMDR,
Eye Movement Desensitization Reprocessing
Certified Level 2 Reiki Practitioner

Major Accomplishments/Recognitions

Executive Director
  San Diego Institute for Bioenergetic Analysis, San Diego,
  California
Local Trainer
  San Diego Institute for Bioenergetic Analysis, San Diego,
  California
International Trainer
  International Institute for Bioenergetic Analysis

Keynote Presentations

The Energetics of Relationships
  2014 Southern California Bioenergetic Conference
Another Story to Tell
  2008 Southern California Bioenergetic Conference

Contact Information

Garet Bedrosian, LCSW, CIRT, CBT, CET
333 Olive St   San Diego, CA. 92103   619.300.8002

garet@garetbedrosian.com
www.garetbedrosian.com

197

Patricia Bucci

Live the Life of Your Dreams

Pat lives her life boldly with passion and deep intention. Serving as a New Jersey educator, Pat taught grades four through twelve and finished her career as a high school principal in 2011.

Pat then moved into the entrepreneurial arena when she founded *Path 2 Success Coaching,* where she works with young people to develop life skills necessary for living an intentional life and pursuing their passions.

Pat also proudly volunteers in the Guardian Ad Litem program, advocating for the best interest of children in the foster care system. She works with Florida's Children's Protective Services and the court system to reunify children with their natural families or, if that becomes impossible, place them in the homes of other loving, caring families.

Finally, Pat has partnered with an international company that develops anti-aging products. In this business, she helps others to feel beautiful inside and out and coaches others in establishing their own businesses in pursuit of their own intentions and passions.

Upon retiring, Pat and her husband moved to Florida where Pat continues to live intentionally and pursue her passion: working with children.

Educational Background

B.S., Education
  Glassboro State College, NJ
M.Ed., Developmental Reading
  Trenton State College, NJ
M.Ed., Educational Leadership
  Monroe, NJ

Major Accomplishments

Teacher: Elementary Middle and High School
Reading Specialist
  Somerville, NJ
H.S. Supervisor and Assistant Principal
  Somerville High School, Somerville, NJ
Principal H.S./M.S.
  Park Ridge High School, Park Ridge, NJ
Path 2 Success Coaching;
  Established to assist young people to develop skills
  necessary to become successful in all areas of life
  Volunteer Guardian Ad Litem Advocate for Children in
  the Foster Care System,
  Lee County, FL
Senior Brand Partner
  Nerium AD, Florida

Contact Information:

Pat Bucci
5386 Christie Ann Place
Sarasota, FL 34233 908-392-0727

www.patbucci.com

199

Marlene Cain

Helping Others Grow

Marcain Communication helps individuals and businesses alike in pursuit of professional growth. Marlene's tools include individual and group coaching, talent acquisition, and professional speaking on career and related topics.

As its founder, Marlene has recruited hundreds of quality candidates for premier companies and coached thousands of employees and job seekers in skills that last them a lifetime. Known as an "entertrainer," Cain is a trained communicator, champion speaker, and award-winning businesswoman who has been recognized at state and local levels for her contributions to business and communications. She currently serves the Big Bear Chamber of Commerce as its chairman.

As an active volunteer, Cain co-founded Bearly Speaking, Big Bear's award-winning Toastmasters Club, and enjoys helping speakers and presenters at any level find their voice. She also credits Toastmasters International® for much of her success.

Cain encourages everyone to keep growing and find the work they were born to do!

Educational Background

B.A., Communications
   California State University,
   Fullerton, Fullerton, CA

Major Accomplishments/Recognition

Recognized for "outstanding commitment...and support
to local businesses."
   California State Senate
Elected Chairman, Board of Directors
Director of the Year: Dedication to the mission of the
Chamber of Commerce
   Big Bear Chamber of Commerce (Big Bear, CA)
Women in Business: Saluting Those Who Make a
Difference
   Big Bear Lake
Professional Expert
    San Bernardino Community College District's
    Professional Development Center
Committee Chair, "Speech Trek," annual speech contest
   American Association of University Women,
Contributing author, Heart of a Toastmaster: From
Toastmaster to Chairman of the Board
   Appointed Ambassador by Toastmasters International
Co-founded"Bearly Speaking"
   Big Bear's award-winning Toastmasters club

Contact Information

Marcain Communication
P.O. Box 6634
Big Bear Lake, CA 92315
Office: 909-866-2819

marcain@earthlink.net
marcaincom@gmail.com

Celeste Ducharme

Believe and Work Hard to Achieve

Celeste Ducharme strives to make the conscious choice to motivate, mentor, encourage, and lead others by example. With a degree in Business Management, and over two decades experience in high-level performance in sales, buying and marketing and management for two high profile companies, Celeste works passionately to create successful, caring, and highly motivated work environments.

People skills and an overall attitude favorable to success are reflected in the myriad promotions offered Celeste over the years. Reaching peak sales and opening new regions for sales and marketing were a natural for this self-driven, self-motivated go-getter who thrives on responsibility and challenge.

Success should be Celeste's middle name! Her skills: managing people, money, and profitability, and sharing success skills with her local community softball program—teaching young girls the art of sports to develop success patterns. If you ask how you can connect with her, Celeste will respond, "With a smile and love!"

202

Educational Background

Bachelor of Science, Business Management
  University of Phoenix
  Phoenix, AZ

Major Accomplishments/Recognition

Female Athlete of the Year 1986
Softball Hall of Fame 1990
  Canyon High School
Le Tip International
President and serving board member—8 years
  Temecula Chapter
Coach of the year 2011-2012
Head Varsity Softball Coach—5 years
Head Travel Softball Coach—7 years
  Calvary Murrieta High School
Sales, Marketing, and Buying—9 years
  Nordstrom
Sales and Marketing Property Manager—10 years
  Clinton Keith Self Storage
Rancon Ambassador—3 years
Wife and mother—23 years

Contact Information

ckss@rancongroup.com
www.HaveFaithAndBelieveBig.com

Susan Kerby

Breathe Through vs. Muscle Through

Susan Kerby is known as an inspirational author, speaker, and trainer. She has been setting stages and hearts on fire with her impassioned message for over thirty years. She is on a mission to help emerging thought leaders find their heart's voice, and align it with their presence and message, resulting in divinely inspired success that changes lives.

Having led over 200 transformational seminars (impacting more than 15,000 lives), and having trained internationally for corporations such as PayPal, StubHub, and Peak Potentials, Susan passes on the magic that leaves your audiences inspired, leaning in, and saying, "I want more; how can I work with you?"

Equally comfortable in five-inch heels as in hiking boots and slippers, Susan cherishes the life of empowerment, adventure, and peace she has created in partnership with her husband, Russ.

Educational Background

B.A., Government and Economics
  Bowdoin College, Brunswick, ME
Transformation and Leadership Training
  Landmark Education Corporation
Thrive Academy
Heart Virtues
Pax Programs Incorporated
Peak Potentials

Major Accomplishments

Designated Seminar Leader
  Landmark Education Corporation
Awarded Circle of Honor
  Outstanding Results and Providing Unparalleled
  Leadership
Chairman of the Board, Los Medicos Voladores
  The Flying Doctors
Honored: Providing "tangible and significant assistance
given for the furtherance of better understanding and
friendly relations among peoples of the world."
  Vision Team, Conscious Business Network

Contact Information

Your Inspired Voice
Santa Rosa, CA
707-953-1242

susan@susankerby.com
www.susankerby.com

Ann Marie Johnson

Confessions of a Leadership Junkie

Ann Marie serves as the Planning and Performance Manager for Chevron's Environmental Management Company. Her role is to build the company business plan, steward safety, and align key company resources with client needs. She has more than twenty years of experience in project management and is a Lean Sigma Black Belt. Ann Marie was a founder of the Chevron Women's Network, which promotes diversity and mentoring for women within the company. Her areas of expertise are in strategic planning, intellectual property management, technology deployment, facilitation and customer satisfaction.

Ann Marie holds a BS in Chemistry and a BA in Sociology from Drake University, along with an MBA from Santa Clara University. She has extensive non-profit Board of Director experience and specializes in fundraising. A married mother of two, Ann Marie enjoys reading and creative writing.

Educational Background

M.B.A.
  Santa Clara University, Santa Clara, CA
B.S., Chemistry
  Drake University, Des Moines, IA

B.A., Sociology
  Drake University, Des Moines, IA

Major Accomplishments/Recognition

Board of Directors
  St. Clare's Christian Preschool
Board of Directors and Secretary
  Loaves and Fishes of Contra Costa
Board of Directors and Fundraising Chair
  San Ramon American Little League
Board of Directors
  Cougar Education Fund
Certificate of Recognition
  California State Legislature (2011)

Contact Information

Ann Marie Johnson
6001 Bollinger Canyon Road
San Ramon, CA 94583

ajohnson@chevron.com

207

Guylaine Saint Juste

Launchpad for Success

Guylaine Saint Juste is the Business Banking Executive at one of the largest banks in the U.S. She provides strategic oversight, cultivates a culture of purpose and significance, and creates a learning organization where a team of professionals can provide good advice and expertise to clients in the emerging market. Her passion is to help her team, her clients, and her community to scale, grow, thrive and prosper.

A thought leader with a keen sense of "perceptual acuity," she is adept at creating a culture of intention and purpose where human capital grows, learns, performs, and contributes. A dynamic, enterprising, and seasoned executive, Guylaine brings broad-based management and leadership experience in retail and commercial banking, talent, operational and organizational strategy development, leadership and implementation of major business lines/units. These skills help her improve performance and profitability, and brand development to deeply enhance value and competitive positioning.

Guy spearheaded the development of a new start-up region; she oversees Small Business strategy for 95 branches, 650 employees, with a deposit base of $1.1B, and total loans of $650M, and leads all aspects of Business Banking including talent acquisition, financial performance, performance management, marketing, and sales.

Educational Background

Bachelor's Degree International Relations
  George Mason University
Graduate Degree, Retail Banking Management
  Consumer Bankers Associations at University of Virginia

Major Accomplishments|Recognition

President and Co-Founder
  Women's Alliance for Financial Education
Past Chair, Court Appointed Special Advocates
  Prince William
Co-Chair, Women's Business Initiative
  George Mason
University School of Business
Board of Directors: DC
Goodwill
  Community Business Partnership
  YMCA Fairfax County
Women Worth Watching,
  Profile in Diversity Magazine
Hispanic Heritage Foundation
  Corporate Leadership Award
President's Award,
  Fairfax Bar Association

Contact Information

guy.stjuste@gmail.com

Victoria Villalba

Leading Out of Necessity

Victoria Villalba is President and Founder of Victoria & Associates Career Services, Inc. Founded in 1992, Victoria & Associates is an experienced group of detail-oriented professionals providing employers with qualified employees to fill interim, replacement, and new positions. We deliver peace of mind through career candidates who add value to your business—as illustrated by our referral history and growing list of long-term clients.

Her career has included work in the area of HR consulting, Recruitment and Staffing within diverse industries. Over the past 23 years, she has served on numerous boards and volunteers with many organizations. Her passion is giving back in South Florida in the community in which she lives, works, and plays.

Victora is blessed with a 26-year-old-daughter and business partner, two four-legged sons (Augie and Alex), two grand dogs (Hijo and Anvil), and resides in Coral Gables, Florida.

Educational Background

B.S., Personnel Management
  Florida Southern College, Lakeland, Florida
M.S., Human Resources
  Nova Southeastern University, Davie, Florida

Major Accomplishments

Director, American Red Cross South Florida
Director, Federal Reserve Bank of Atlanta
  Miami Branch
Director, PACE Center for Girls
  Miami-Dade County
Director, Greater Miami Chamber of Commerce

Contact Information:

6100 Blue Lagoon Drive
Suite 355
Miami, Fl 33126

Victoria@VictoriaAssociates.com
www.VictoriaAssocia

Want More Opportunities to Stay Connected?

Sign up to receive Lisa Marie Platske's e-zine

The Upside Thinker provides you with opportunities to:

Connect with other movers and shakers—and difference makers;

Attend Upside Chats, free monthly training interviews with business experts who share thousands of dollars of content-rich information to accelerate your results;

Be motivated every Monday with Lisa Marie's weekly Upside Thought of the Week filled with inspiration, tips, and resources, designed for the busy professional.

Subscribe now to receive all the above and much more at no cost to you!

To sign up, please
visit www.UpsideThinking.com

Connect in person at one of our LIVE Upside Events

Leadership Success Summit

Upside Thinking, Inc.'s signature two-day annual conference that brings hundreds of business professionals together to map out a step-by-step plan for the upcoming year to increase revenues, and build long-lasting connections.

For details:
http://www.LeadershipSuccessSummit.com

Dare2Share Experience

A boutique connection event that teaches participants how to turn contacts into contracts to grow their business, increase their bottom line, and develop lasting business partnerships.

For details:
http://www.DaretoShareEvent.com

Thank you!

...for reading *Turn Possibilities Into Realities*. We trust you have not only enjoyed these rich stories, but will find some of them inspired you to find a different perspective on your own life and leadership. Thank you in advance for taking the time to post a review for the book on Amazon; many readers will not take that "step" to purchase and read... until they know someone else has "led" the way.

http://bit.ly/ReviewPossibilities

Also available in digital format! on Kindle:

http://www.amazon.com/dp/B00UKEG4RE

Lisa Marie Platske

Other Books by the Author

Designing Your Destiny - *Achieving Personal and Professional Success Through Upside Thinking*

http://www.amazon.com/dp/1934379069

http://bit.ly/PlatskeDestinyBarnesNoble

Connection: The New Currency - *How Everyday Women Collaborate to Build Wealth, Community, and Prosperity*

http://www.amazon.com/dp/0615505929

Made in the USA
Middletown, DE
17 March 2015